The Big Little War

*The incredible story of how a handful of RAF pupil pilots
and their instructors saved Britain's Middle East empire
in 1941 - and why they were excised from history.*

James Dunford Wood

*Published by
Kensington Square*

For Colin,
and in memory of all the other pilots and crew who fought,
and in many cases died, in Habbaniya in May 1941.

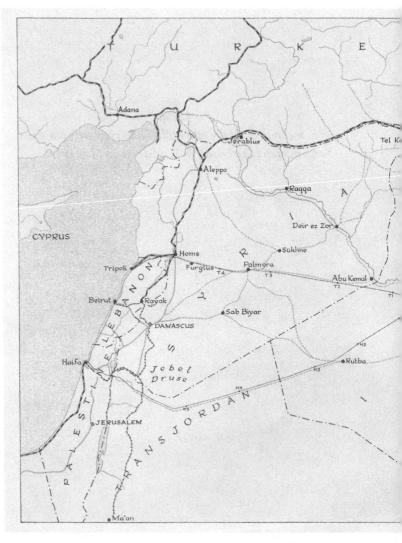

A map of Iraq, Syria, Palestine, Lebanon and Transjordan in 1941, showing Habbaniya just to the west of Baghdad, and the railway running through northern Iraq to Syria.

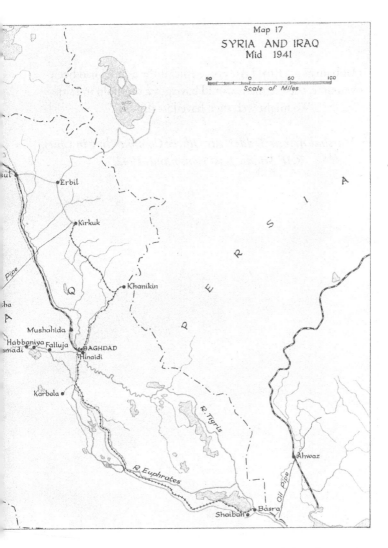

Map 17
SYRIA AND IRAQ
Mid 1941

Scale of Miles
50   0   50   100

A line from Kirkuk shows the oil pipeline running to Haditha, where it splits into the T branch, to supply the French in Tripoli, and the H branch, to supply the British in Haifa.

"Habbaniya is a Royal Air Force epic. If the School had been overcome, the Germans would have got a foothold in Iraq. We might well then have lost this war."

Air Marshal Arthur Tedder, Air Officer Commanding in Chief, RAF Middle East Command, 1942.

Contents

Introduction

I FIRST CAME ACROSS THE NAME HABBANIYA as a 14 year old schoolboy. I can remember lying on the floor behind a sofa, surreptitiously leafing through the pages of a tattered, hard-cover diary inscribed 'India - Iraq 1939-42'. My father's handwriting was barely decipherable, but the entry headlined 'Habbaniya, May 2nd, 1941' was every bit as gripping as my current bedtime reading, 'Biggles Goes East'. It sounded thrilling:

> *"War! I went up at sunrise in the back of Broadhurst's Audax, without a parachute like a fool."*

What was an Audax? I was determined to find out.

The diaries came in several volumes, and had lain gathering dust for years. No one had spoken of them in the family, and certainly not since my father had died of a sudden heart attack at the age of 52. Yet one day, scanning the single bookshelf we possessed for something to read, I came across three stained, battered notebooks. The first sported a sticker announcing its provenance as the 'Indian Stationery Store, Madras'; the second was held together by faded blue duck tape; while the cover of the third was warped with water damage. Each had an old strip of black Dymo embossed with the relevant years from 1939 to 1947, and every other page was pinned or clipped with maps, photographs, letters and press clippings. It was as if I had stumbled across my father again, three years after his death, waiting to tell me of his adventures, his fears, his high points and his lows.

My father had had what his contemporaries called a 'good war', and he had the medals to prove it. The diaries covered multiple well known theatres - the North West Frontier, Burma, Egypt and the Rhine - plus one that was little known to the schoolboy historian, a place called Habbaniya, in Iraq. What I read about it, and in particular a series of twenty-eight diary entries that covered May 2nd-31st 1941, was astonishing. So as soon as I could, I went to the library to see what I could find out about this place. Amazingly, there was nothing. Nor did any of his medals reference Iraq. So I quizzed my history teacher, who shrugged his shoulders and replied: didn't I mean Iran? These were the days before Google. I drew a blank. The diaries went back on the shelf. I returned to Biggles.

Perhaps that was where they would have stayed, had it not been for a news article many years later which described Coalition forces coming across a desecrated British war cemetery in the aftermath of the First Iraq War in what was then known as Camp Habbaniya. Under the rubble, and the weeds, and the smashed headstones, lay the bones and ashes of over 100 British aircrew and army personnel who had been killed at the RAF station there in May 1941. I recognised two of them - Ian Pringle and Pete Gillespy - as names which cropped up on practically every page of my father's diary entries between January and May 1941. Hooked once more, I retrieved the diaries from their shelf and began to read them in earnest. With the arrival of the internet, research material was a bit more plentiful than it had been when I was a teenager. But what I discovered was no less amazing.

It had all started in April 1941 when an Iraqi politician named Rashid Ali had staged a coup with German support and marched on the RAF training base at Habbaniya. Iraq at that time was an ally of Britain's, providing the British with a crucial stepping stone in their lines of communication between India and Egypt. On top of that, most of the oil that the Empire ran on - including, crucially, Britain's Mediterranean fleet and her army in North Africa - was sourced out of Basrah in the south. Habbaniya had been chosen by the RAF as a place to train fledgling pilots on the basis that it was safe, far from the front line. Nothing, supposedly, ever happened there.

The timing could not have been worse for the British. In early 1941 they were fighting alone against the Nazis. To the east, they faced a pincer movement in the Mediterranean that threatened Egypt and the Suez Canal. General Wavell, C-in-C Middle East, who was responsible for defending over a million square miles with, initially, just 100,000 troops, had had some early successes against the Italians in Operation Compass in Libya over the winter of 1940/41, and for a while he was hailed a hero in the British press. But the honeymoon was short lived. In February Erwin Rommel's Afrika Korps landed in Tripoli, and before long Wavell had ceded the bulk of the territories he had won from the Italians, his army forced back to the borders of Egypt.

Meanwhile across the Mediterranean the Germans had begun building up forces in Romania and threatening Greece, and in March 1941, at the behest of Churchill, 50,000 of Wavell's troops - troops which could barely be spared in the face of Rommel's advance - were sent to aid the Greeks. To add to his pressures, Wavell was also fighting on a third front: to the south, in Ethiopia, his forces were still battling the Italians.

This was the situation at the end of March 1941. In early April, it suddenly, and dramatically, worsened. On 6th April two British generals, Neame and O'Connor, were captured by a German patrol in the Western Desert. On the same day, the Germans launched their invasion of Greece and the Greek army fell back, forcing the British expeditionary force onto the defensive. In little over a week they were having to evacuate by sea. On 11th April, Rommel began the siege of Tobruk. Capturing it would have meant being able to resupply his forces by sea and would give him a realistic chance of reaching Cairo and removing the British from the Middle East entirely.

Into this maelstrom, while fighting desperately on multiple fronts, Wavell was confronted by a further crisis: Iraq. In addition to marching on RAF Habbaniya and threatening Wavell's lines of communication with India, Rashid Ali had also cut the oil pipeline from Kirkuk to Haifa. All the British had in theatre to resist the Iraqis was a rag-taggle of superannuated old biplanes and training aircraft. The flying school there could muster just thirty-nine pilots - instructors and pupils - and some threadbare infantry elements, mostly Assyrian camp guards. It amounted to a very 'thin red line.' To make matters worse, rumours were reaching Wavell and the War Cabinet in London that preparations were underway to send Luftwaffe units to reinforce the Iraqis via Vichy French held Syria.

The scene, then, was set for one of the most remarkable battles of the Second World War which, had it been lost, would have crippled Britain's power in the Middle East. If Iraq and its access to the Persian oil fields had fallen to the Germans, Syria would not have been far behind, and Wavell could hardly have held out in Egypt. If Egypt and the Suez Canal had fallen, how could Britain have carried on, and how would American public opinion have reacted? Even if she had struggled on until Pearl Harbor and the Americans had joined in the war against the Nazis, the advance up the Italian peninsula would not have been possible. Without it, the D-Day landings would have faced much stiffer opposition.

As I soon discovered, of all the battles of the 20th century, there has never been a more underreported campaign that had such strategic significance. There was also a very good reason why I had been unable to find an Iraq medal amongst my father's collection - no campaign medals had ever been awarded to the trainee pilots and crews who saw most of the action, despite a casualty rate of over thirty percent. Why was this, and why had the official history glossed over the episode? This book seeks to answer those questions, as well as to finally shed light on an incredible story of heroism and ingenuity in the face of a seemingly impossible situation that, had it failed, could have altered the course of the war.

Prologue

Pilot Officer Colin Dunford Wood was nervous as he waited in the Operations tent with the rest of the aircrew, a few minutes before dawn, some fifty-five miles to the west of Baghdad. He was about to step into the observer's seat of a Hawker Audax biplane and go into action for the first time. Even at this hour, the air was already thick and heavy, nearly seventy degrees, warming up for another scorcher of a May morning. A grey smudge was beginning to stain the darkened sky over the desert to the east.

'The Butcher' - Group Captain Savile - read out their orders, tapping with his stick on the wall map where Iraqi gun emplacements were marked in thick red chinagraph pencil. There were likely to be many more, the C/O informed his young students and their instructors standing wherever they could in a wide semicircle around him. But as soon as they were airborne and the first bombs dropped, he pointed out cheerfully, the Iraqis would be sure to open up on the camp, and the flashes in the half light of dawn would make it much easier to pinpoint them. Altitude for the Audaxes was to be maintained at under 2,000 ft, and bombs released at two hundred feet before pulling out of the dive. They were to keep a watch for the little Italian Fiat tanks, which could 'bite' if you strayed too low. He ended with a ringing message from the Prime Minister that had been received earlier via the camp's wireless transmitter: *'If you have to strike, strike hard.'*

Dunford Wood hadn't slept a wink during the short night, yet was wide awake. Just seven hours earlier he and his fellow pupil pilots and their instructors of the No. 4 Service Flying

Training School (4 SFTS) of RAF Habbaniya had received the news that they were to attack, without warning, at 05:00 the next day. Beyond the main aerodrome, which was in full view of the enemy, was a steep escarpment overlooking the camp. On top of it, unseen in the darkness, lay 9,000 Iraqi troops, with, by one estimate, over two dozen field howitzers, a squadron of Italian built tanks, fourteen Crossley armoured cars, and numerous machine gun posts. Dunford Wood's recce flights during the last thirty six hours - first flying a Hart trainer over the Plateau the day before, and then twice that day in an Audax, had confirmed the build up. Not far beyond them, fifteen minutes away by air, was Hinaidi air base on the outskirts of Baghdad, where there were the best part of ninety aircraft of the Royal Iraqi Air Force, trained into a formidable fighting machine by military advisors paid for by the British Government. The irony was, they had far better machines than the flying school could muster. Those advisors had now been withdrawn, some fleeing to the camp at Habbaniya, others to the embassy in Baghdad, where they now slept on lawns and in the ballroom under virtual house arrest.

He was nervous, but excited. It was, after all, what he had signed up for, having recently transferred to the RAF with three other junior officers from the Indian Army. Little had he realised, when he had put in for the move, that the 'sleepy backwater' he was being posted to, would turn out to be anything but quiet. He couldn't believe his luck. Here was some real action at last.

Some of his superiors, a mix of ex-flying club instructors and semi-retired RAF pilots, felt otherwise. It was one almighty cock-up as far as they were concerned, for hadn't the powers that be, seen this coming? Everyone else had. And why hadn't they been reinforced from Delhi, or from Cairo? The only help that had arrived were several hundred troops of the King's Own from India, who had been airlifted in from Karachi via a series of staged hops, and six clapped-out Gladiator biplanes, which were apparently all that General Wavell, C-in-C Middle East, could spare.

So now here they were, a few moments before 05:00, about to clamber into an assortment of superannuated old training aircraft: lumbering dual control Airspeed Oxfords (top speed 192 mph), painted yellow; fabric covered Hawker Audaxes, long since retired from active service in frontline squadrons; and some ancient Fairey Gordon bombers. Until recently very few of these aircraft had had any bomb racks, and they had had to be hastily customised in the preceding weeks in a frantic race to become combat ready, with, in the case of the Oxfords, some ill fitting metal brackets which had yet to be tested properly, certainly in action. There was some concern, and plenty of grim humour, as to whether their clutch of 20 lb bombs would survive the bone-shaking rattle of take off, and not fall to the ground and blow up their hosts before they could become airborne.

The worst of it, however, were not these 'string bags', as the aircraft were referred to by their long-suffering pilots. It was the pilots themselves. Of the thirty-five instructors, only three had actually seen any active service, and they would soon have to be supplemented by the four ex-Indian army officers who had passed their elementary exams - part one of the course - just two weeks earlier. They were known, amongst themselves at least, as the 'Four Musketeers'. None of the four had had any formal training in air to air combat. As for the crews, there were just two trained observers, and two trained gunners. The rest were pupils.

As they climbed aboard the machines and checked the fuel levels and the ammo belts, few of the older hands imagined they would survive more than a day - two at the most. All the Iraqis would have to do, once they had recovered from the surprise of this preemptive attack, would be to walk into the camp. Who could stop them? Not the Assyrian Levies, the local camp guards, who numbered about 1,200. Although they hated the Iraqis with a vengeance and could probably be relied upon to slit a few throats, they were no match for 9,000 professional Iraqi soldiers who, like their air force, had modern equipment that Britain's servicemen could only dream of. And the 360 or so British troops of the King's Own would fare little better.

Even if the Iraqis preferred to wait it out, one hit on the water tower or the electricity plant would spell the end for the camp, as Dunford Wood's superiors knew only too well. Yes, RAF Habbaniya was state of the art, but it had certainly not been built with combat in mind. With its well laid out boulevards, its club houses, its boating lake, its polo ground and acres of oleanders, it was a cushy posting far behind the front line, the ideal place to teach new recruits to fly. Normally some redundancy would have been planned for - a back up water tower, an auxiliary electricity plant - above all, an aerodrome that was not outside the main camp and overlooked from the high ground beyond. But this had not been considered necessary when the camp was built six years earlier. Iraq had only recently been run by the British under a League of Nations Mandate, with an Anglophile royal family, and was still bound by a treaty of mutual friendship which promised aid in time of war. In other words, Iraq was supposed to be a firm ally. Or rather it had been, until the military coup that had swept Rashid Ali to power four weeks earlier. The Regent had had to be smuggled out of Baghdad to Habbaniya in his pyjamas, in the boot of the American Ambassador's car.

So the camp was the proverbial sitting duck. All that stood in the way of the besieging Iraqis and a humiliating capitulation was 4 SFTS. As the first aircraft revved prior to take off, hooded torches directed them towards the airfield gate in the perimeter fence, to sneak out in line, one by one. The grey dawn had now spread out from the East, and shapes on the edge of the desert were just becoming distinguishable. Waiting his turn, Dunford Wood patted his pocket one last time, to make sure of his Goolie chit[1] in Kurdish and Arabic, and adjusted his specially adapted goggles, without which he was practically blind in this half light. Then he turned his attention to the first world war vintage Lewis machine gun he was in charge of in the back seat. It was prone to a series of stoppages when it got hot, and was notoriously moody. As he checked the ninety-seven round pan magazine and eased the breach open, it snapped back and caught the edge of his index finger. He uttered an expletive and heard his pilot, Broughton, shouting through his earphones to remind him to belt on his parachute. Dunford Wood had forgotten it, 'like a bloody fool', as he was to write in his diary the following day.

It was the beginning of one of the most incredible battles of World War Two.

~

1. Named from the Hindi word for ball, Goli, the Goolie chit was a 'blood chit' that offered a reward for helping a downed airman, so named for the tendency of rebels on the North West Frontier to castrate captured non-believers. The operation was typically carried out by the women, and there had been stories in Iraq of similar treatment at the hands of the tribes.

Part 1

A Secret Meeting

Nine months before that dawn takeoff in the half light at Habbaniya, a secret meeting had taken place between an Iraqi Justice Minister and the German Ambassador to Turkey in Ankara. That city had long been a hotbed for spies.[1] As a neutral country, Turkey hosted the legations of the various warring parties, whose staff would mingle freely in the bar of the Park Hotel next door to the German embassy. Both the British and the Germans were seeking to recruit the Turks to their cause, so far without success.

In early July, a man named Naji Bey Shawkat travelled by train from Baghdad for a medical procedure. Or at least that was the official reason for his visit, but as the German ambassador Von Papen reported back to Berlin afterwards, the Iraqi Minister for Justice came with an urgent message from his prime minister, Rashid Ali.

Shawkat opened the meeting by apologising on behalf of the Iraqi Government for breaking off diplomatic relations with Germany the previous year, and lamenting the absence in Baghdad of their long time friend and supporter, the former German ambassador Dr Fritz Grobba. It was not something they should have done, he said, it had been carried out by an earlier prime minister, Nuri el Said, at the behest of the British, and as Von Papen should be aware, Ambassador Grobba and Germany were held in high esteem by his government in Baghdad. But now, he said, the British were pressuring Rashid Ali to break off diplomatic relations with the Italians, who had entered the war just a few weeks earlier.

The basis on which the British were making these demands of the Iraqi government, as von Papen knew, was the Anglo-Iraqi Treaty of 1930, which had been signed following the end of their Mandate to govern Iraq. This was an arrangement that had been put in place by the League of Nations following the fall of the Ottoman Empire - of which Iraq had formed a part - after World War One.

This treaty was one of friendship, alliance and mutual support in time of war. Because, despite the ending of the Mandate, Britain retained considerable influence in Iraq and, crucially, the treaty granted them rights to two air bases, one in Basrah, the other in Habbaniya. The former protected the supply of oil to Britain from the Iranian and Iraqi oil fields, while the latter provided an important way station along the imperial lines of communication between Egypt and India.[2]

Notwithstanding the treaty, Shawkat informed von Papen confidentially, Rashid Ali was refusing to do Britain's bidding, despite pressure from pro-British elements in his Cabinet. Nonetheless, Shawkat said, his government had no faith in the Italians, who in his opinion were even more untrustworthy than the British. So he had come to ask for German help for a co-ordinated uprising across Iraq, Syria and Palestine. In particular he urged the ambassador to ask Berlin for a public statement in support of their pan Arab aspirations. His government was keen to act as soon as possible, in view of the expectation that the British would soon take over Vichy controlled Syria. Given Britain's weakness, just six weeks after Dunkirk, would not this be an ideal moment to strike, he asked?

§

It was not an unreasonable request, in the circumstances. Iraqi-German ties had been growing steadily since the early 1930s, largely as the result of a very proactive policy pursued on behalf of the German government by their former ambassador, Dr Fritz Grobba. It was Dr Grobba's efforts in the years leading up to the war, before he was expelled, which had led to some expectation amongst the Arabs that Germany would support their cause, which was to create a pan-Arab Caliphate, free of colonial control, from the Mediterranean to the Arabian Sea.

Fritz Grobba was a fascinating character. Classically Aryan with fair hair and blue eyes, he was portly from a surfeit of good food and wine, gregarious, charming, and a prolific and generous host. He spoke excellent Arabic and was an experienced Middle East specialist who had served in Palestine during World War One and, in the 1920s, as Germany's first envoy to Afghanistan. His network of friends and contacts in Turkey and throughout the Arab states was unrivalled, and proved very useful to his superiors in Berlin. He was also respected by them, and by the Arabs themselves, as being one of only a few in the German diplomatic service who truly understood the Arabs and their cause. Despite the traditional reluctance of Berlin to get involved in the Middle East, Grobba was keen to foster a closer relationship between Germany and Iraq, seeing a real opportunity to advance Germany's interests in the world at the expense of Britain and France.

His work in Iraq had begun in 1932 when he had arrived in Baghdad, post-Mandate, as the first German ambassador to the newly independent country, and he had quickly set about fostering high level contacts in the Iraqi military, in particular with a group of four pro-German Iraqi colonels who would become known as the 'Golden Square'. These officers had started their careers in the Ottoman Army, which in the period prior to the First World War had been trained and equipped by Germany. But it was more than training that they received - they were also indoctrinated into a culture of military nationalism, developing a close affinity with their German mentors. After all, Germany provided a very relevant role model, having formerly been a mix of states and principalities which all shared a similar cultural and racial heritage, before coming together as one nation just fifty years earlier. These idealistic young nationalist Arab army officers could see clear parallels with their own situation.

Grobba had a decent war chest in gold and sterling from his government to aid his work, so at his behest, and Germany's expense, dozens of young Iraqi army officers were sent from Baghdad to Berlin for training throughout the 1930s, despite this being in contravention of the Anglo-Iraqi treaty, which stipulated that any military training for the Iraqi army should be the preserve of the British. In addition, in 1936, 150 Iraqis had been given invitations to the Olympic Games in Munich, and in 1937 the Iraqi Director General of Education visited Germany and an agreement was struck that enabled Iraqi students who studied German to be offered free educational placements in German universities. The same year, senior Iraqi medical officials were given an official reception in Berlin, and in 1938 an Iraqi delegation attended the Nuremberg Rally.

To further boost German influence in Iraq, Grobba set about having extracts of Hitler's *Mein Kampf* translated into Arabic, and in order to make sure it reached a wide circulation, he arranged for the German embassy to buy a local daily newspaper as a vehicle to publish these extracts. The paper's circulation grew. Soon everybody in Iraq was reading *Mein Kampf*, and Germany's stock amongst educated Iraqis began to rise. When Grobba invited the head of the Hitler Youth, von Schirach, to visit Baghdad and talk about his new German youth movement, Schirach proved to be a huge draw for younger Iraqis, and it was not long after the visit that an Iraqi youth movement, *Al-Futuwwa*, was launched, modelled on German lines, to join the Iraqi Nazi party that had already been started by German expatriates.

With all this activity, it would be natural to suppose there was a carefully planned strategy within the German Foreign Ministry to undermine the British in Iraq during the 1930s, and indeed there were a number of high ranking Germans who supported

Grobba in his aims. However, the strategy was not well embedded, and the visits and relationship building were largely the initiative of Grobba. Hitler, after he came to power, showed little interest in affairs outside of the European theatre, and as the 1930s wore on, his ministers followed his lead. Indeed, he had a particular disinclination to get involved with colonial independence movements, for two reasons.

First, from his racial perspective, Arabs were an inferior race on a par with the Jews. In an effort to sway the Fuhrer in the early days, a number of those who shared the views of Grobba had introduced Hitler to various Egyptian and Indian nationalist leaders. Hitler wrote that he found them *"pompous asses full of verbiage but devoid of any solid foundation in reality,"* and that he was irritated that even in the Nazi camp there were Germans *"who let themselves be taken in by Orientals with such an inflated sense of their own importance."* He was simply not interested in collaborating with colonial peoples oppressed and exploited by the British, whether Arab or Indian.[3]

A second reason was down to his admiration for the British. Like his own people, Hitler considered the British to be an Aryan race, and his strategy once he came to power - and even after war broke out - was to try to seek an accommodation with them. For allowing him carte blanche in Europe, and support for the unification of the German 'volk' under a single national banner, he was ready to allow Great Britain a free rein in the rest of the world, to run their colonies as they chose.[4]

Official German government policy in 1940, then, was at odds with the efforts that representatives like Grobba had made to foster a relationship with the Arabs in the run up to the war.

§

So Von Papen's eventual reply, having heard Shawkat out, was cagey. He reiterated his government's policy that any initiatives in the Middle East should be led by Germany's ally, Italy. This was the result of an agreement known as the Ribbentrop-Ciano Pact which had been signed earlier in the year, that gave Italy the lead in all Arab matters, given that she had colonies in Libya and East Africa.

Following the Ankara meeting, a circular was immediately sent around German embassies and legations in the Balkans and the Middle East, reminding them of Axis policy, and setting out how Arab overtures like the one Von Papen had received should be handled: cautiously. No commitments should be given, and the Arabs should be told that *"Germany pursues no political interests in the Mediterranean ... and will therefore let Italy take the lead in the political reorganisation of the Arab area."* [5]

When Shakwat returned to Baghdad empty handed, his government might be forgiven for feeling like a damsel who has been led up the garden path to be, at this critical juncture, spurned at the altar.

~

1. In the next decade Ankara was to be the backdrop for two of the most infamous spies of the 20th Century - a German spy of Albanian origin called 'Cicero', and the Russian spy Kim Philby, both of whom were working as spies within the British embassy, the former as a chauffeur, the latter as the station head of intelligence.

2. The Anglo-Iraqi Treaty that followed the end of Britain's League of Nations mandate over Iraq was signed in 1932. The two air bases were to be newly built at Habbaniya and Shaibah (outside Basrah) after the RAF ceded their two existing air bases, at Hinaidi in Baghdad, and Mosul, to the new Iraqi Air Force. The Treaty also stipulated that the British would have the right to transition troops through Iraq.

3. As Hitler wrote in Mein Kampf in a passage that Grobba pointedly did not translate into Arabic, it would be "impossible to overwhelm, with a coalition of cripples, (in other words the oppressed peoples), a powerful state that is determined to stake, if necessary, its last drop of blood for its existence. As a völkish man, who appraises the value of men on a racial basis, I am prevented by mere knowledge of the racial inferiority of these so-called oppressed nations from linking the destiny of my own people with theirs."

4. Hitler was always an admirer of the British Empire. What was called his Englandpolitik was fully in sync with the racial tenets of National Socialism, which visualised a world under white Germanic and Anglo-Saxon domination.

14

5. Documents on German Foreign Policy 1918–1945 (Washington, D.C.: Government Printing Office, 1957), vol. 10, p. 515, document 370, Circular of the Foreign Ministry, 20 August 1940 - quoted by Gossman.

*'The Four Musketeers' - Allan Haig, Ian Pringle,
Colin Dunford Wood, Pete Gillespy.*

The Four Musketeers

As cables were flying back and forth between German embassies
in the Middle East and the Foreign Ministry in Berlin, events were
unfolding in other theatres of war that would soon converge.

In India, far from the front line, Second Lieutenant Dunford
Wood was frustrated. Having graduated from Sandhurst in
1938, he had been posted to the 1st Battalion, the Leicestershire
Regiment, known as the 'Tigers', where he had had his first taste
of action on India's North West Frontier. As a callow 20 year old,
it was exciting stuff, as he recorded in his diary, exactly what he
had signed up for, fighting against Pashtun rebels led by the
Osama bin Laden of his day, a tribal chief called the Fakir of Ipi.

In fact a posting to the North West Frontier after graduation from Sandhurst was considered to be a very lucky posting indeed for an ambitious young officer.

The days had been filled with recce patrols into the hills, rotaing in and out of fortified picquets, and sporadically being sniped at by marauding tribesmen. In the summer of 1939, the going was pleasant and the nights were cool, but as the winter came on, the hills had become barren and icy, and most of the time was spent cooped up in camp. Every month a letter would arrive from his old school friend Bill Robinson, who was with the 2nd Battalion, King's Own Royal Regiment, 2,500 miles to the west in Palestine. Robinson seemed to be doing exactly the same thing, patrolling the hills around Jerusalem, trying to avoid snipers and roadside bombs, though in his case they could equally well have been planted by Jews as by Arabs. It was confusing, as Robinson confessed, unused to being hated so universally by both sides, but neither of these two young subalterns spent much time thinking about politics. Such was imperial policing across the British Empire as war broke out in Europe.

Dunford Wood remembered the moment it came, vividly, as he huddled around the radio with his fellow junior officers in the wilds of Waziristan to listen to Chamberlain declare in sombre tones that since *'no such undertaking has been received...this country is at war with Germany.'* Their first reaction was to get drunk. Their second was to dream of some proper fighting, anywhere other than India. Three weeks later Dunford Wood was posted to an Indian army regiment, the Frontier Force Rifles, in Madras, and, as he lamented in his diary, *'yet further from the War do I go.'*

It was certainly not dull in Madras, with its endless rounds of cocktail parties, cinema outings, sailing and dancing, and the occasional duck shoot at weekends - but it wasn't war. His brother Hugh, back in Britain, was flying Blenheim bombers in 21 Squadron and was soon to see action in the Battle of France. As 1939 turned into 1940 with a drunken party at the Adyar Club in

Madras where, Dunford Wood reported, *'the only drawback was the Governor's band,'* prospects did not look that good for ambitious Indian army officers.

A few weeks before Christmas he had decided he would learn to fly, and signed up for lessons at the Madras Aero Club, with a vague notion that if nothing developed, he would seek a transfer to the RAF to join his brother. It certainly seemed to offer a better guarantee of action. As the months wore on and the social whirl of Madras ground on, he gradually learnt how to spin, roll and dive, flying antiquated but sturdy Tiger Moths. In June his brother was reported as missing on a bombing run against German armour over northern France, and in the late summer Dunford Wood was posted to a training battalion. Finally his mind was made up. As he wrote in his diary in September 1940:

> *'It's getting cold here now and depression, mental and physical, is setting in. I don't seem very fit these days, I must say, and nothing ever happens, one day succeeding another.'* [1]

It was time to make a move. Initially his request to transfer was denied by his commanding officer, *'the old shite.'* But he didn't give up, and in October a message came through, out of the blue, that Indian army officers were invited to apply for secondment to the RAF, and he was to report to Air HQ in Delhi for an interview and a medical. He was not hopeful, however, because his eyesight was poor, and the civilian pilot's licence he had been issued with by the Madras flying club had an addendum *'subject to correction of vision.'* In practice this meant some specially adapted goggles with lenses in place of clear glass. Still, he harboured hopes of being accepted as a navigator even if he failed his medical as a pilot.

He explained what happened next in his diary:

> *"I mention my eyes and they all look grave. I am*

*walking around the quad, looking at the pretty typists
(it's the Nizam of Hyderabad's palace) when I see the
Medical Officer's room, and Haig on his exam – I also
see the eye test board, so I write it down, (it seems to
be a gift – "never look a gift horse in the mouth" etc.),
memorise it, and am passed as 6/6. How long it will
last I don't know. I reckon I will be pushed out after a
few weeks, or even days...*

*Our course is six weeks at Drigh Road, Karachi, then 4
Air Training School, Iraq. Off tonight on the Frontier
Mail to Lahore and then on to Karachi – the great
deceit – how long will it last – and will I be court-
martialed – Quien Sabe?"* [2]

Haig was Allan Haig, another Indian Army officer looking to
transfer to the RAF, along with two others who Dunford Wood
met that day - Pete Gillespy and Ian Pringle. For Gillespy, it was
third time lucky. The first time he had tried to transfer he had been
turned down. The second, he had taken matters into his own hands
and deserted, travelling to Bombay to try to stow away on a ship
bound for home to join up back in the UK. Eventually he had been
caught and court martialed as AWOL, but now, finally, he had got
his wish.

After six weeks training in Karachi and some hastily snatched
Christmas leave on his uncle's tea plantation in Assam, Dunford
Wood embarked with his fellow trainees - now calling themselves
'The Four Musketeers' - by ship for Basrah in Iraq. They arrived in
late January 1941 and transferred to the training school at RAF
Habbaniya. As he described in his diary on arrival, *it's a happy and
relaxed station, far from the front line'.*

How happy, and how relaxed, the Four Musketeers were soon
to find out.

~

1. The War Diaries of Colin Dunford Wood, Vol. 1, September 1940.
2. The War Diaries of Colin Dunford Wood, Vol 1, 28th October 1940.

General Archibald Wavell, 1938.

Wavell

WHILE THE MUSKETEERS were steaming west towards Iraq, letters from home painted a mixed picture. Britain was still in the grip of the Blitz, and heavy Luftwaffe raids continued on provincial cities such as Bristol, Liverpool, Plymouth and Cardiff. But what the papers were full of that grim winter were General Archibald Wavell's successes in North Africa, in Operation Compass against the Italian 10th Army.

After the Italians had declared war on Britain in June 1940, they had made a limited advance into Egypt. In December, despite being numerically outnumbered almost five to one, Wavell's forces counter-attacked, and in five days had driven the Italians back into Libya. In the beginning of January they captured 40,000 Italian troops at Bardia, and just two days before the Musketeers landed in Basrah en route to Habbaniya, British and Australian troops completed their capture of Tobruk. By the end of the first week of February they had overrun most of Cyrenaica, Libya's eastern province, to the Gulf of Sirte, halfway to Tripoli. The operational commander on the ground who led the advance, General Richard O'Connor, famously messaged Wavell after he had trapped the Italians at Sirte, following a daring dash across the desert to cut off their retreat along the coast road, *"Fox killed in the open."* [1]

While the British suffered fewer than 2,000 casualties, they captured over 130,000 prisoners, the bulk of the Italian 10th Army, including three generals. It was a resounding success, the first great land victory of the war, and a huge psychological boost for the British. It also helped to raise Britain's stock around the world, for the balance of the war was just then on a knife edge, and a number of important neutral countries were weighing up their options. Most important of these were the Americans, where a large majority of the population was against getting involved, a view that was reinforced by the seemingly hopeless position of Britain.[2]

Turkey was also important, as their involvement could hold the key to control of the Eastern Mediterranean. Last, of course, were the Arab and Indian subjects of the British Empire. Any failure by the British was likely to embolden the rebellious nationalists amongst them, and Britain could ill afford having to deal with any fifth columnists across her dominions in time of total war.

So Wavell was lionised. As so often happens in the darkest days when things are at their bleakest, successes are leapt upon, and Wavell was quickly dubbed by the British press 'the Victor of Bardia'. In truth, much of the credit was due to his commander on the ground, General O'Connor, but nevertheless Wavell was acknowledged as one of Britain's top generals, not least by the Germans.

However, Operation Compass was just one of the many moving parts Wavell was having to contend with. Of all the posts held by British political and military leaders at this stage in the war, Commander-in-Chief Middle East was arguably second only to the Prime Minister. The responsibilities and stresses were enormous, and very few military leaders would have been up to the task.[3]

For example on his appointment in August 1939, Wavell commanded all British land forces not just in Egypt, but also in Palestine, Sudan, Transjordan and Cyprus. A month later, as war was declared, he was also given responsibility for Iraq, Aden and British Somaliland. Together, this amounted to over three and a half million square kilometres at the heart of Britain's empire, a land bridge between Britain's far eastern possessions and the Mediterranean, Gibraltar and home. In addition to command of all land forces, Wavell's instructions were to build and maintain close co-operation with the various political leaders and government authorities across his command, whether governors, high commissioners or ambassadors, as well as those of Britain's ally France in the region - which meant Algeria, Tunisia, Lebanon and Syria. His role, effectively, was to be that of a kind of Imperial proconsul, wearing a political as well as a military hat. Last, he was to liaise with Britain's considerable naval and air assets in the Mediterranean, as well as with the armed forces of allies France and Greece.

Ranged against him were the armies of Italy's African empire, based to the west in Libya, and to the south in Ethiopia and Italian Somaliland.

Wavell, then, had a lot to contend with, and spent much of his time shuttling back and forth between the various capitals on ancient RAF transport planes. To counter the Italian threat across this vast area, he had hardly enough troops to maintain order, let alone resist a determined attack. For example, when war broke out, he had under 50,000 troops, made up of one incomplete armoured formation, twenty-one infantry battalions, two cavalry regiments still on horseback, four artillery regiments with sixty-four artillery pieces, forty-eight anti-tank guns and eight anti-aircraft guns, plus a few more locally raised troops in British Somaliland, Aden and Kenya - the latter not strictly under his command. Against this paltry force, the Italians could field 300,000 troops in the region.[4]

One of the first things Wavell did was to lobby London for more troops and equipment, though with everything being thrown into the Battle of France, and subsequently the defence of Britain herself, there was little to spare. By the Spring of 1940 he had been reinforced with two brigades from India, two from Australia, one from New Zealand, and the 1st Cavalry Division from the UK, which was sent to garrison Palestine. Once Italy joined the war in June, he persuaded Churchill to send tank reinforcements, including a regiment of the heavyweight Matildas, which at the time were state of the art. His position in the Middle East had become particularly vulnerable with the French out of the war and their troops in North Africa and Syria now under the control of the Vichy government. This was a brave act by Churchill, considering that Britain was in the midst of the Battle of Britain and expecting invasion at any moment. But it came at a cost. Wavell's visit to London in August 1940 to ask for these reinforcements was generally considered disastrous on a personal level, as it was clear that Churchill and Wavell, two very different characters, did not see eye to eye. It was from this moment that the Prime Minister's doubts in his Middle East commander began to grow.

But for the moment Wavell was untouchable. The success of Compass against overwhelming odds deserved all the praise it was given in the British press. However, events soon conspired against him: Germany entered the fray. For the Italians had not only fared poorly in North Africa - they were also faltering in Greece, against whom they had launched a disastrous invasion in October 1940. Within three months, as Wavell's forces were trapping the Italian army outside Sirte, the Greeks had reversed the Italian advance and were pushing them back into Albania.

Despite their victories though, the Greeks were soon struggling. Without the manpower to rotate troops in and out of the line, they were unable to capitalise on their advance, and as Italian reinforcements were brought in across the Adriatic to stem the tide of their advance, they urgently sought help from Britain.[5] Churchill was also receiving worrying reports via the 'Ultra' intelligence decrypts about the appearance of German forces in Romania to support the Italians.[6] So he made a fateful decision. He cabled Wavell on 10th January, just five days after the capture of Bardia and while Operation Compass was still raging:

> *"Destruction of Greece will eclipse victories you have gained in Libya, and may affect, decisively, Turkish*

attitude, especially if we have shown ourselves callous of (the) fate of allies. You must now therefore conform your plans to larger interests at stake...all operations in Libya are subordinated to aiding Greece..."[7]

This left Wavell in a quandary. Urged on by his frontline commander, O'Connor, he was keen to continue the advance into Libya while he had the Italians on the run, and if he had been allowed to do so beyond the middle of February, he would likely have captured Tripoli and sewn up the whole of the country. This would have denied the Axis powers any ports to the east of Tunis and so make it very hard for reinforcements to be sent from Europe. But there were several other factors he had to consider. First, his lines of communication were now severely stretched. In this new form of desert warfare, water and petrol had to be provisioned over hundreds of miles. Second, his hardware had taken quite a beating from the unfamiliar desert conditions they were fighting in. Tank tracks had become clogged and broken, engines overheated, guns seized up, and there was a severe lack of spare parts. Third, now that the Italians were beaten, it was estimated that it would take at least four months for them to be able to build up their forces again and mount a counter attack, so in the meantime, if push came to shove, eastern Libya could be held by a scratch force. And there was a very big push, not to say a forceful shove, coming from Whitehall, in the direction of Greece.

So despite the rocky relationship Wavell had with Churchill, it's easy to see why he did not initially push back on these demands. At the very least, he was prepared to go to Greece to find out what they needed. Ironically, the very next day, on 11th January, Hitler issued his *Directive 22*, which provided both for the reinforcement of the Italians in Albania, and for the swift despatch of forces to Tripoli under Erwin Rommel. The Ultra decrypts had accurately foreseen the former. No one predicted the latter.

On 13th January Wavell flew to Athens to confer with the Greek prime minister and his army commander, General Papagos. The talks were inconclusive. The Greeks wanted nine British divisions, but Wavell could only spare two, so for the moment nothing was decided, and his forces were left free to continue their advance into Libya. Operation Compass thundered on. On the 22nd Tobruk fell, and more Italians were taken prisoner. Meanwhile, far to the south, other elements in his Command were advancing against the Italians in Italian East Africa, which now included British Somaliland which the Italians had annexed on the outbreak of war. On the 28th, Wavell flew to get an update from his commanders in Sudan and Kenya, and on his return to Cairo he cabled London that his forces were going to exert 'maximum effort' to conquer Italian East Africa throughout February and March.[8]

By this point, two British divisions had vanquished ten Italian ones in Libya, and Tripoli was his for the taking.

However, the Greeks continued to badger Churchill, and their case was reinforced by the Ultra intelligence that was now showing a continuing, and massive, build-up of German forces in the Balkans. At a Defence Committee meeting in London on 10th February the pros and cons of advance in North Africa versus reinforcing the Greeks was discussed. As Churchill minuted, it would be 'wrong to abandon' the Greeks. The next day Wavell was informed, and told that a definite decision had now been made. He must switch his priorities, and *concentrate all your available resources in the Delta in preparation for movement to Europe*.[9] When the Chief of the General Staff, General Dill, expressed his doubts that any troops could be spared from Egypt, aware of the huge risk in the operation, Churchill lost his temper, *'What you need out there is a Court Martial and a firing squad. Wavell has 300,000 men!'*[10]

It was a huge exaggeration, given that many of these 'men' were not frontline troops, but then Churchill was not one to let niceties like that get in his way. From a tactical point of view, it was a big gamble. But from a strategic point of view, it was unavoidable, as Britain could not be seen to abandon her allies, and public opinion in the US - so important for the future direction of the war - would not forgive inaction. It was this that in the end swayed Wavell to support the plan where so often before he had resisted Churchill's sometimes hare-brained instructions. It was also seen as a way to draw Yugoslavia and Turkey into the war alongside Britain to support the Greeks, and Anthony Eden was sent to Cairo to try to engineer such an alliance. He left London on the 12th February.

The same day, the first elements of Rommel's Afrika Korps landed at Tripoli. For the first time the phlegmatic Wavell began to feel uneasy.

~

1. Coincidentally another 'fox' - Gaddafi - was killed in the open at the same spot almost exactly seventy years later.
2. In a Gallup survey in January 1941, for example, the American public had been asked "If you were to decide on the question of the United States entering the war against Germany and Italy, how would you vote — to go into the war, or to stay out of the war?" 88% said stay out.
3. Wavell had been just fifty-six at the outbreak of war, and had already had a stellar career. After being wounded at the 2nd Battle of Ypres in WW1, where he lost an eye and was awarded the Military Cross, he had been posted to General Allenby's staff and had entered Jerusalem with him in 1917 alongside T.E. Lawrence. So he had first-hand knowledge of the 'Arab problem'.
4. The Crucible of War, Barrie Pitt, p5.
5. This they were entitled to do, under a military guarantee that had been given by Britain and France following the annexation of Albania by Italy in 1939.
6. Germany was keen to secure the oil fields in Romania to support Operation Barbarossa against Russia in the summer.
7. Wavell, Soldier and Statesman, Victoria Schofield, p167.
8. Cable to Dill, reported in Wavell, Soldier and Statesman, Victoria Schofield, p 170.
9. Wavell: Soldier and Statesman, Victoria Schofield, p 171.
10. As reported by Dill, quoted in The Business of War, John Kennedy.

A Happy and Relaxed Station

PILOT OFFICER COLIN DUNFORD WOOD's first impressions of RAF Habbaniya when he arrived were favourable. He wrote in his diary on 3rd February:

> *"The road out here is 60 miles across flat, open plain, and 20 miles of nothing, not even road, across Fallujah Plain – a pukka sand desert! Habbaniya is a camp well laid out, rather similar to Wana or Razmak, but more vast and better organised. Training here are a lot of Greeks and South Africans, and they had Norwegians and French before we arrived. We are the only four*

officers on this course, the rest being other ranks from Kenya and Malaya.[1] We fly Harts. Up at 6, flying until 9, breakfast and lectures until 12.30. Then next day lectures until 10 and fly until 12.30 – and so on, alternately.

Went racing yesterday, first time since Blighty. A very nice boat club here on Lake Habbaniya, where the flying boats come down. I went out on a whaler..."[2]

The attraction of this sleepy backwater was immediately apparent. The peace and tranquillity of the desert was considered an ideal place to teach new RAF recruits to fly. More importantly it was safe - both politically, and on account of the flat terrain to cushion the inevitable forced landings that befall many newbie pilots. The RAF's training school, 4 SFTS, had transferred here from Egypt in 1939.[3]

The man in charge was Acting Air Vice-Marshal Harry 'Reggie' Smart. Smart lived up to his name, at least sartorially, and was a stickler for rules and routine, the perfect candidate to oversee a flying school. Short, slim and dapper, he had started his career in the Royal Flying Corps in the First World War, but for the last eighteen years had been a flying instructor and aeroplane tester. His responsibilities now were rather wider. As the AOC (Air Officer Commanding) of British Forces in the area, his primary role was to keep Iraq open as an air and land bridge through which Imperial forces could transit. Multiple plans had been put in place, and war gamed in Whitehall, with playful operation names such as *Heron, Herring, Lobster* and *Sabine*, to move reinforcements from India to Palestine, Palestine to Iraq, Egypt to India, and so on, depending on the strategic requirement. To this end, supply dumps, staging posts and landing grounds needed to be maintained at a number of locations throughout the Iraq to connect the seaport of Basrah with neighbouring Transjordan and Palestine. The most significant of these staging posts was RAF Habbaniya itself.

Smart was also tasked with helping to work up a plan to advance into Iran from Iraq should war break out with Russia, which was considered a realistic possibility in Whitehall after the signing of the Nazi-Soviet non-aggression pact in 1939. Several recce flights were flown from Habbaniya to Baku, to assess the feasibility of bombing Russia's oil fields in the area should the need arise.

However, for the moment his new Command was far from the front line, and the expectation was that it would remain that way. His background as a flying instructor was considered ideal. The team of instructors he oversaw were a mix of civilian flying club trainers in uniform, with no military background, and various ex-operational RAF pilots no longer required on, or suitable for, the front line.

And what a station it was. A military cantonment on the Indian model, it had twenty-eight miles of tarmac road bordered with oleander[4] and eucalyptus, pepper and casuarina trees, with names reminiscent of home - London Gate, the Strand, Piccadilly, Regent Street - and of RAF aces - Sefton-Baker, Salmond and Ball. It boasted a country club, a cinema, a fully equipped hospital, three churches (Anglican, Armenian and Assyrian), acres of manicured lawns, and playing fields for rugby, football and hockey; a golf course and a polo pitch in the centre of the camp; stables for ponies; and even its own pack of hounds, which was called the Royal Exodus Hunt.[5]

Finally there was a sailing club on nearby Lake Habbaniya with a clubhouse and bar, next door to a comfortable Imperial Airways rest house (it became BOAC in late 1939) where massive, whale-like Short Empire flying boats on their way to and from India and Egypt could land, refuel and overnight. At the centre of it all stood Air House, a luxurious white villa that was the residence of the

AOC - *'where electric fans stirred the air lazily and the footfalls of booted warriors were deadened upon soft Persian carpets.'*[6]

Indeed, there was ample well-appointed accommodation both for the British residents as well as for the locally enlisted staff and militia, the 'Assyrian Levies', whose job it was to guard the base. Finally, there was a large open air swimming pool, a state-of-the-art gym and fifty-six tennis courts.[7] It housed, in total, 9,000 people, and was nicknamed the 'Jewel in the Desert'.

It sounded like the perfect posting. However, in reality it had a number of drawbacks. For a start, the climate was oppressively hot for much of the year, and the area was prone to vicious sandstorms.

As Dunford Wood wrote in his diary some weeks later, Habbaniya *"is in the middle of a desert and dust storms make life bloody. The Euphrates runs alongside and last year the camp was evacuated to the Plateau above the lake as there was a danger of the river bursting the bund."* Unlike in India, there was no cool and refreshing hill station that servicemen could escape to for a bit of R and R. It was also a male only station - postings were unaccompanied - so other than the AOC's family and a few nurses in the hospital, no female company was to be found. The men had to drive fifty-five miles across the desert to the fleshpots of Baghdad for that.[8]

The safety of the location was also deceptive. Two crucial factors made this base different from many others the British military had constructed elsewhere in the Empire. Being supposedly a friendly country, where a treaty had just been signed, and for reasons of cost, it was considered unnecessary to duplicate essential facilities for water and power, making the base extremely vulnerable should they be put out of action.

Second, the airfield itself was left outside the seven mile camp perimeter fence. A gate in the fence gave access to the hangars. It was laid out on the bare desert, on packed sand, with no bomb-proof shelters, no dispersal areas and no defensive arrangements of any kind. It could be seen for miles around, and was overlooked from the 150ft high escarpment of the Fallujah Plateau. As for the perimeter fence itself, this had been designed purely to *'keep out wild animals and marauding Bedouin',*[9] and in no way was a proper defensive structure.[10]

Nevertheless, Dunford Wood and his fellow Musketeers were unaware of these security shortcomings. As far as they were concerned, three months learning to fly at Habbaniya was a welcome, if sometimes uncomfortable, break from other theatres of war, and a lot more interesting than pointless parade ground exercises in India.

For training, 4 SFTS had three types of aircraft. At the entry level were a number of Hart trainers - customised versions of the Hawker Hart light bomber, with all the armaments stripped out and dual controls fitted in the front and rear cockpits. Once a pupil had learned to fly on the Hart, they graduated to one of the station's thirty Hawker Audax biplanes, this time without dual controls, which could also be used for practising bomb aiming, gunnery and message-pick-up, using a hook attached under the fuselage. These too were a variation of the Hawker Hart design, also principally used as light bombers, and they had been the RAF's plane of choice for controlling the tribes in the region during the Iraq Mandate. The planes had a .303 fixed and synchronised Vickers machine gun in the front, manned by the pilot, and a drum operated Lewis gun, ring-mounted in the rear cockpit. Under the wings they could carry eight 9 lb practice bombs on specially mounted racks.

For instruction in navigation, wireless operation, range finding and instrument flying, pupils were taken up in the station's fleet of twenty-seven Airspeed Oxfords - nicknamed the Ox-box - which had been produced from 1937 to cover a wide range of training requirements, and mostly used in the UK for training the pilots and crew of Bomber Command. To denote their training status, they were painted bright yellow, and could be seen well before they could be heard. They also carried camera equipment, so could be used to learn aerial photography. These twin engined

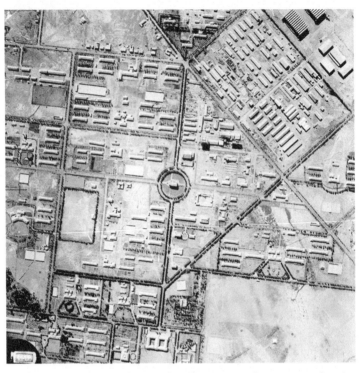

An aerial view of RAF Habbaniya, showing Air House (the camp's HQ) at the bottom edge with the polo ground to its right.

monoplanes were made from wood and plywood and could seat a crew of three. Like the Harts, they had dual controls, as well as a full array of instruments. Unlike the Harts, they carried sixteen practice bombs.[11]

In addition to the training aircraft of 4 SFTS, RAF Habbaniya had a handful of obsolete and lumbering Fairey Gordon biplane bombers, used for towing targets for gunnery practice, and three Gloster Gladiators. Even though the Gladiators had only been in service for four years, they were the last biplane fighters to be produced in the role for the RAF, and were already being superseded by the new monoplanes, the Spitfire and the Hurricane. Like the

Audaxes, their twin .303 Vickers machine guns were synchronised to shoot through the propeller blades. The three planes were left over from when the base had been a front line station, before the training school took up residence, and were reserved as stylish runabouts for the station's senior commanders.

Finally, there was a Communications Flight of three large Valentia biplanes, modified versions of the earlier Vickers Victoria Bomber, used for transport tasks.

Other than that, the only other RAF planes in Iraq were twelve old Vickers Vincents belonging to 244 Squadron based four hundred miles to the south at RAF Shaibah near Basrah. They were also used as transporters.

As February turned to March, rumours reached the camp of political manoeuvring in Baghdad. The prime minister, Rashid Ali, had been removed from power earlier in the month, to be replaced by a pro-British minister, but it didn't seem like it was a popular move in the bazaars of Baghdad, and British military personnel were starting to report a hostile atmosphere. On the 22nd February Dunford Wood reported a conversation with the camp's intelligence Officer, Wing Commander Jope-Slade, who told him some 'interesting things about Iraqi politics'.

Nevertheless, nobody seemed too concerned, and the four Musketeers settled down to a comfortable routine. Most of the flying was done before lunchtime, for at this time of year, the temperature was bearable. By the early summer nothing would move after 11:00 in the morning. Flying practice was interspersed with lectures given by one of thirty-five instructors at the school. The afternoons were free, and the ex-Indian army officers alternated between swimming in the club, sailing on the lake, shooting jackals in the desert, and the occasional football match. Dunford Wood also bought a share in a polo pony, after some haggling with its previous owner, who was being posted away to Egypt, and he rode her out on the bunds, raised embankments that protected the plains from the seasonal flooding of the Euphrates.

The social life, despite the absence of women, was varied. There was a regular rotation of new faces and officers from British military units far and wide, as they transited through Habbaniya on their way east to India or Singapore, or west to Egypt and Palestine. They brought news of adventures from other theatres of war, and the evenings could be long and drunken - whisky before dinner in the club, more booze afterwards, and the inevitable difficulty the next morning when attempting to fly 'straight and narrow'.

Nor was it only the pupils who got drunk. The senior officers and instructors, many of them not much older than their students, also joined in the fun. A typical afternoon in early March followed the promotion of the Chief Flying Instructor, 'Larry' Ling, to Wing Commander, as recorded in Dunford Wood's diary:

> *"They all celebrate in style. At about 4pm, all pickled, they make for the hangars, Levies and all, and away in the air. Luckily only one plane is crashed, landing on the polo field, but there are acrobatics near the ground, inverted circuits and God knows what. Cremin (one of the instructors) was the worst. Too pissed to convince anyone he could fly, he is taken in the back of an Audax with no parachute, and trying to bail out all the way. And coming back the same."* [12]

Training was divided into two parts - the Intermediate course, which was passed after sixty-five hours flying (including night flying) and exams in groundwork; followed by the Advanced course, which involved gunnery and bomb practice, aerial reconnaissance and photography, and message-pick-up. At the end of March, with only a few hours to go to pass his Intermediate, Dunford Wood had a scare. He had survived the eye test in Delhi by cheating, but he could only manage to fly by wearing a pair of specially adapted flying goggles with prescription lenses. Like standard goggles, they had darkened glass as protection against the glare, and since all pilots wore similar goggles in the open cockpits to prevent the wind blinding them, it was easy to get away with. But he had not factored in a new skill that had to be learnt.

> *"We were night flying and before starting, my instructor Garner says 'be sure and use these plain flying goggles', handing me a pair – I think Christ, put them on my helmet and, when in the cockpit, I change them over for the pair with the lenses that I bought in Karachi. Then through the earphones comes:*
>
> *"Are those dark bloody goggles you are wearing?"*
> *I say yes, and I prefer them, but he makes me change them, stuffing my own pair in my pocket. So off we go, with me quivering and wondering how the hell I shall be able to see the signal light."* [13]

If his poor eyesight was ever discovered, he knew he would be thrown out of the RAF and sent back to the Indian army. As he wrote later, it had been a very 'close shave'.

~

1. One of the students from Malaya was Tom Slack, who described events at Habbaniya in *'Happy is the Day - a Spitfire pilot's story.'*
2. The War Diaries of Colin Dunford Wood, Vol 1, 3rd February 1941
3. The spot chosen for the base following the Anglo Iraqi Treaty of 1930 was a practical one - near enough to Baghdad for supplies to reach the base the same day, but far enough to be left undisturbed by Iraqi politics. It took five years to build, and when the base became operational in 1936 it was 'state of the art' for comfort and efficiency. However, by the late 1930s life had become so quiet in Iraq that there was barely any operational flying undertaken by the RAF in Iraq at all. Part of their original mission had been to pacify the rebellious Iraqi tribes, and, post-Mandate, to train a new Iraqi Air Force so that they could do it themselves. Mission accomplished, the squadrons stationed there were now required elsewhere, and so in 1939, just after the outbreak of war, they were transferred to Egypt, and 4 SFTS, the training school, was transferred in the opposite direction to replace them, in accordance with a pre-existing plan. Only a communications

flight of three Valentia biplanes to transport freight and personnel was retained from the previous establishment, along with an engineering depot.

4. Habbaniya in arabic means *'of the oleander tree'.*

5. One of their hunting horns famously turned up in the rubble of Arnhem in 1945, having belonged to a British officer who had been a former hunt member.

6. The Golden Carpet, Somerset de Chair, p 55.

7. The War That Never Was, Tony Dudgeon, p. 20.

8. Roald Dahl, the British writer who had been learning to fly here just six months before Dunford Wood arrived, remembered being told he was being posted to *"the most god forsaken hell-hole in the entire world",* which he described afterwards as *"a vast assemblage of hangars and Nissen huts and brick bungalows set slap in the middle of a boiling desert on the banks of the muddy Euphrates miles from anywhere...It was beyond me why anyone should want to build a vast RAF town in such an abominable, unhealthy, desolate place..."*

9. Britain's Informal Empire, Silverfaub, p 130.

10. Concerns had been raised as early as 1933, as construction was starting. Lord Hailsham, the Secretary of State for War, had questioned the *"difficulty and dangers of extricating the RAF in the event of trouble in Iraq."* Lord Londonderry, the Secretary of State for Air, replied that *"so long as the Anglo-Iraqi Treaty was in effect, no hostile act by the Iraqi Government against our forces could reasonably be contemplated."* Lord Hailsham's letter to Lord Londonderry, and Lord Londonderry's reply, 10th and 12th October 1933.

11. The aviator Amy Johnson had died piloting an Oxford in the UK just a month earlier.

12. The War Diaries of Colin Dunford Wood, Vol 1, 15h March 1941.

13. The War Diaries of Colin Dunford Wood, Vol 1, 15th March 1941.

Some Interesting Things
about Iraqi Politics

WHAT WERE THESE 'interesting things about Iraqi politics' that Dunford Wood referred to in his diary entry for 22nd February? And what had happened to oust Rashid Ali from power, he who had so recently been seeking German help to throw out the British?

To understand what was going on in the Spring of 1941, we need to briefly go back to the start of Britain's involvement in Iraq, to the break-up of the Ottoman Empire at the end of World War One.

In 1914, although the Ottoman Turks controlled less than half of the territory they had ruled over in their heyday at the end of the 17th century, it still extended to the borders of Persia and covered most of the Middle East. When World War One broke out, the Turks sided with the Central Powers, Germany and Austro-Hungary, against the British, French and Russians. This opened up an opportunity for the Arabs, for so long under the yoke of the Ottomans, who suddenly found themselves courted by both sides. There had already been discussions between the leader of the Arabs, the Emir of Mecca Sharif Hussein, and Lord Kitchener, then the Vice-consul of Egypt. Kitchener had wanted to know whether the Arabs would support Britain in any war against the Turks, and for his part, Hussein wanted British protection against the growing encroachment of the Turks into Arabia by means of a new railway they were constructing to link Constantinople with Mecca.[1]

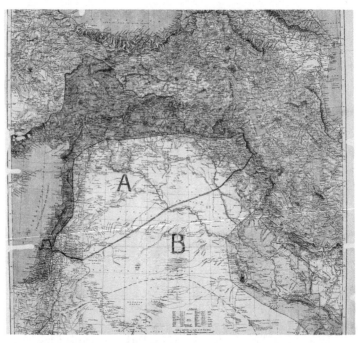

The infamous Sykes-Picot map, showing proposed zones of control and influence for the French (A) and the British (B).

So Hussein was already sounding out the British. At the same time he was being pressed hard by the Turks to make his forces available to support them against the Allies. Then, soon after war broke out, a Turkish plot to oust Hussein from the throne as Emir of Mecca was uncovered, and as a result, in 1915, he sent his son Feisal to meet with Arab dissidents in Damascus to coordinate action against the Turks. These dissidents had long held a vision of a pan-Arab caliphate centred on Syria, and they wasted no time in urging Feisal to ask his father to join them and lead the revolt. Feisal soon realised, however, that they were too weak on their own, and would need Great Power support. So they drew up the 'Damascus Protocol', declaring that they, the Arabs, would revolt in alliance with Great Britain in return for recognition of Arab independence in an area running from the southern border of Turkey, to Persia and the Persian Gulf in the East, and south by the Arabian Sea - pretty much the entire area under Ottoman control south of Turkey.

Eventually an undertaking was given, in an exchange of letters between Sir Henry MacMahon, who had replaced Kitchener as the High Commissioner in Egypt, and Hussein, in October 1915. Effectively it was a written commitment, backed by the British Government, to support the creation of an independent Arab state.[2]

One man in particular was pleased with this outcome: T.E. Lawrence. Soon to be lionised as 'Lawrence of Arabia', he was working for British military intelligence in Cairo at the time, and was already a vocal supporter of the Arab cause and a champion of their right to self determination.[3]

Lawrence was also keen to support the Arab revolt for another reason. Just a few months after this letter was sent, he became aware of parallel, though separate, negotiations with the French on life after the Ottomans, which culminated in the secret and soon to be infamous Sykes-Picot Agreement. This sought to carve up the Arab lands of the Ottoman empire into spheres of influence marked on a map with a red crayon for the British and a blue one for the French. In so doing it clearly acknowledged French designs on Syria and only referenced the Arabs' rights to an independent state in the vaguest of terms, which, because it was to have as its capital Damascus, was left entirely at the discretion of the French. It seemed that Britain - more than living up to her reputation as 'perfidious Albion' - was promising to support the acquisition of the same tract of Ottoman territory to two different entities. For Britain's part, she would get control over Mesopotamia, which subsequently became Iraq, and the oil supplies that flowed through Basrah. The Arab cause, it seemed, was in danger of being sold out for oil. Lawrence knew that the only way for the Arabs to prevent it was by changing the facts on the ground, and fighting the Ottomans themselves.[4]

This contradiction soon came to a head. After the defeat of the Ottomans in the First World War, Lawrence pushed for Feisal to be rewarded for his support by being made the first king of a new, independent state of Syria. Unfortunately, as a result of the Sykes-Picot agreement, the French had other ideas. In April 1920 the League of Nations - dominated by the victorious allies, and in accordance with Sykes-Picot - had granted mandates to Britain and France to administer the former Ottoman territories, on condition the arrangement was temporary and that they were not be be treated as colonies.[5]

France's mandates would be for Syria and Lebanon, while the British were to be responsible for Palestine (which included Transjordan) and Iraq. The British hoped that the French would come to a reasonable accommodation with Feisal, whose supporters were bitterly opposed to the Mandate. France, however, wasted no time in giving Feisal an ultimatum - get his supporters to accept it or be forced out. The resulting Arab revolt was crushed by the French in a short campaign. To the dismay of the British, it became clear that the French intended to treat their Syria mandate very much as a colony after all.

A wave of Arab discontent rippled out across the Middle East, leading to violent unrest across British administered Iraq. Within months the revolt had tied up over 100,000 British and Imperial troops and had cost the lives of 877 British servicemen and the impoverished exchequer £35 million.[6] It looked as though administering Iraq was going to turn out to be a very costly, and very bloody, exercise.

It is not clear whether it was the British Colonial Secretary of the time, Winston Churchill, or Lawrence himself, who came up with the clever idea of swapping one throne for another and making Feisal King of Iraq. But it was clear to all that the region was in a mess.

The Arabs were further angered when they realised that the 1917 Balfour declaration, under which the British promised to support the creation of a Jewish homeland, would actually become a reality now the British had the Mandate for Palestine.

So Churchill decided to hold a conference to try to 'straighten the tangle', as Lawrence put it. Held in Cairo in March 1921, it brought together the British governors of the various territories plus all the relevant military leaders and their advisors, including Lawrence. What emerged was an ingenious solution: the British would offer their mandated territories to the two sons of Hussein. Abdullah would be offered Transjordan (part of the Palestine Mandate), while the recently deposed Feisal would get Iraq. Their father Hussein would continue to rule Arabia. Each would get a subsidy from the British government, and so if one misbehaved, they would all suffer. This, it was hoped, would encourage them to keep each other in line, it would defuse the French-Arab conflict, and it would honour the spirit, if not exactly the letter, of the McMahon agreement.

Feisal was an inspired choice. As the leader of the Arab revolt against the Ottoman Empire of 1916-17, and as a direct descendant of the Holy Prophet, he was much respected, despite not having set foot in Iraq before becoming king. It also removed him from any possibility of leading a new revolt against the French in Syria.

Lawrence's thinking was that it would also lend legitimacy to the two new states, but in a way that was consistent with the Mandate, as they would be supported by British funds as well as administrative expertise. To cement Feisal's legitimacy, a plebiscite was organised across Iraq. This consisted of a single question with no alternate choices: voters were simply asked if they professed allegiance to Feisal or not.

Not surprisingly Feisal was elected King with 96% of the vote.[7]

Still, Feisal's job was not an easy one. Iraq was a melting pot of tribes, nationalities and cultures, Shia and Sunni, that had never been ruled as a single homogeneous territory by the Turks. On the one hand Feisal had to deal with a hothead section of urban society who had not given up their dream of a pan-Arab caliphate, and who felt cheated by the British, and on the other he had to contend with independent tribal sheikhs who could see little difference between rule from Baghdad and rule from Constantinople. However, well respected as he was, and with the support of the British, Feisal proved remarkably successful throughout the 1920s in keeping Iraq together and in forging the institutions of this new state.

To support him, the British agreed to bolster the new administration with a number of RAF squadrons. This was both a cost effective solution, and a much more discreet method of enforcement, as ground troops would always look like occupiers.8 The six month revolt was brought swiftly under control, allegedly by the dropping of phosphorus bombs and tear gas.9 The tribes had never seen an aeroplane before and fled at the sight of them, and suddenly a new and cost effective method of control was born that, it was estimated, would save up to £20m a year for the UK Treasury.

Twenty years later, Feisal was dead, but the RAF was still in Iraq, and the senior British commander in the region was the RAF officer running Habbaniya's flying school. The days of bombing the tribes were long gone. So were the means, and all that remained in the air were those antiquated old biplanes.

~

1. The Hejaz railway was an ambitious project to speed up the political and economic integration of Arabia into the Ottoman empire, allowing the Turkish army to move their troops vast distances over the desert to assert control over the Arabs.

2. The agreement was hedged around with various caveats,particularly concerning the Mediterranean coastal areas, where Arab influence was weakest, and McMahon also made clear that the Arabs should seek help and advice from the British alone when setting up their new administration.

3. Nine months later, in June 1916, Hussein launched the revolt with Lawrence as Britain's liaison officer, earning him his famous title, Lawrence of Arabia.

4. Cartographers and their maps have long been the handmaidens of empires. They were used by imperialists to carve up territory with a stroke of the pen, and the fruits of their labours are still scattered across the globe. The Sykes-Picot map

and the agreement to which it was attached was the prime cause of rising Arab discontent against the British in the 1930s, and its after effects still reverberate today.

5. The American President Woodrow Wilson insisted that these Mandates be granted for a limited period only, until the Arabs could stand on their own feet as independent nations.

6. R.M. Douglas, The Journal of Modern History, Vol. 81, No. 4 (December 2009), pp. 859-887.

7. As Churchill wrote to Sir Percy Cox, the High Commissioner for Iraq in Baghdad, *"Western political methods are not necessarily applicable... and the basis for election should be framed."* Winston's Folly: How Winston Churchill's Creation of Modern Iraq led to Saddam, Christopher Catherwood, p97 - (Churchill to Cox 12/1/21).

8. The RAF had already proved their worth in a recent revolt in Somaliland led by the 'Mad Mullah', where the Army had been unable to send the two divisions that would be required for a ground offensive. The Air Chief Marshal at the time, Lord Trenchard, suggested that he could do the job far more cheaply with two squadrons of the RAF. This 'junior service' had only been in existence for a few years, and was keen to prove its worth. Instead of large and expensive ground forces, Trenchard argued that small contingents of his new fighters and light bombers could be used to 'fly the flag' and, as a last resort, bomb the rebels into submission. He was allowed to test his theory in Somaliland, and so it proved. Now the strategy was extended to Iraq.

9. Did Britain Use Chemical Weapons in Mandatory Iraq? R.M. Douglas, The Journal of Modern History, Vol. 81, No. 4 (December 2009), pp. 859-887 Douglas shows that it was unlikely that chemical weapons were actually used, although they were authorised by the Colonial Secretary, Winston Churchill, until an international treaty banned them soon after.

Rashid Ali al-Gaylani, Prime Minister of Iraq, March 1940 - February 1941 and April - May 1941. He was also Prime Minsiter briefly in 1933.

Rashid Ali

IN THE AUTUMN OF 1940 rumours started to reach the British that the Iraqi government was trying to forge closer ties with Germany. There is no evidence that they knew of Shawkwat's meeting with von Papen, but they were getting intercepts of Italian radio traffic from Baghdad to Rome, through which messages to Berlin were conveyed.

As far as the British Foreign Office was concerned, prime minister Rashid Ali had to go, and as had been the case so often in the past when they needed changes made in Iraq, they turned to their most loyal supporter, the Iraqi monarchy, in this case the Regent, Prince 'Abd al-Ilah. Al-Ilah had been appointed Regent just before war had broken out, to rule on behalf of Feisal's grandson, three year old Feisal II. He was another anglophile in Feisal's mould, but unfortunately with none of his authority.

Indeed, since Feisal's death in 1932 the power of the monarchy in Iraq had been steadily eroded by the rise of the Iraqi Army. While Faisal had been alive, he had been able to maintain control, and because he owed everything to the British, he could always be trusted to serve Britain's interests.[1] However, his son and heir, Prince Ghazi, proved nowhere near as accommodating, nor as level headed. Twenty-one years old when he succeeded to the throne, Ghazi was a playboy who had been bullied at Harrow, which didn't bode well for the British. A racy moustache took the place of his father's more formal goatee, and being of the new generation, he had a love of fast cars and Hollywood movies, and was susceptible to the new shiny Fascist ideology that was being broadcast across the world from Europe and championed by the glamourous new German ambassador, Fritz Grobba. But he had none of the unifying presence of his father, leaving a vacuum that was to be increasingly filled by the Iraqi Army as the 1930s progressed. Socially, he mixed with the new generation of forward looking young army officers, who he had trained with at the Baghdad military academy for three years just before acceding to the throne. They brought with them new ideas, and were followers of the tight knit military group who Grobba had been cultivating, the 'Golden Square'.

Grobba was quick to curry favour with Ghazi too, and it was during Ghazi's rule that German influence began to ratchet up in Iraq. This coincided with a growing instability amongst the various ethnic groupings in Iraq, which led to a series of Army coups, launched to maintain order where Ghazi could not.[2]

An accelerating drumbeat of coup and counter-coup throughout the 1930s was followed with concern in London, and for a while, according to Foreign Office papers, the British were considering the feasibility of forcing Ghazi to abdicate. His tone was becoming increasingly anti-British, especially in the public support he was voicing for the Palestinians, just then in the middle of their uprising against the British Mandate in Palestine and the rapid influx of Jewish emigres. In addition Iraq, if anything, was becoming of even greater strategic importance, following the completion of an oil pipeline from Basra to Haifa on the Mediterranean coast a year ahead of schedule in 1934.

Indeed the Palestinian revolt, and Britain's hard-line reaction to it, did a great deal to cement anti-British feeling across the Middle East in the 1930s. In Iraq, attacks were made on the new Kirkuk-Haifa pipeline, and King Ghazi took up the cause via his private radio broadcasts. The Iraqi army, too, was sympathetic.[3]

But by the time war broke out, Ghazi had gone. On 3rd April 1939 he was killed in a car accident, in suspicious circumstances. He had driven his open top Buick head on into a telegraph pole en route between his radio station and his palace in Baghdad, and the police report was perfunctory. Stirred up by German propaganda, many in Iraq believed it had been a British plot, and there were riots around the country, which in Mosul led to the murder on the steps of his residence of the British consul, Gordon of Khartoum style. Whatever the circumstances - and it was almost certainly an accident - it was clear that the choice of the Regent to look after his heir, three year old Feisal II, his anglophile uncle Al-Ilah, was engineered by the British.

There was an outpouring of grief across the country, with Ghazi posthumously lionised as a hero of the pan-Arab and Palestinian cause. As had happened with his father, Ghazi's sudden death dealt another body blow to Iraq's fragile stability. The Regent was weak, having little in common with the Arab nationalist army officers, nor any particular political acumen or understanding of what the role involved.[4]

As 1939 unfolded, Germany's rise in the world order did not go unnoticed, particularly amongst the four Iraqi Colonels of the 'Golden Square'. They quickly came to prominence as leaders of the Nationalist, anti-British and pro-German clique. When Germany invaded Poland in September 1939, they arranged for film footage to be shown to awe-struck Baghdadi audiences.

Soon after, a new and malignant actor appeared on the Iraqi stage. In October 1939, a month after war was declared, the leader of the Palestinian revolt, the Grand Mufti of Jerusalem, long a thorn in the side of the British administration in Palestine, was forced by the French to flee Lebanon, and he went straight to Baghdad, to be followed by a succession of Palestinian and Syrian exiles. This might have been seen by the British as a satisfactory result at the time, keeping him away from the troubles in Palestine, but in reality, as events would show, it simply served to switch the focus of Arab agitation eastwards. The Grand Mufti was now seen as the unquestionable leader of the Arab cause and he was immediately welcomed in Baghdad as a hero. His hennaed goatee gave him the nickname 'The Red Fox'. [5]

The Red Fox wasted no time in setting up an official committee of Arab nationalists in Baghdad with representatives from Syria, Palestine, Transjordan, Saudi Arabia, along with the four Colonels of the Iraqi army. Also included in this group was the nationalist Rashid Ali. Just as the British had presented the Arabs with an opportunity to rid them of their Ottoman overlords in 1914, so the outbreak of a Second World War now gave the Arab nationalists in Baghdad a new opportunity: Germany could help them throw out the British. Strategic considerations were shifting. It was now Iraq, and Baghdad, that became the centre of Arab nationalism. Together with the Red Fox, Rashid Ali and the Colonels began to plot in earnest about how to exploit the new world order.

As 1939 drew to a close, the British ambassador in Baghdad, Sir Basil Newton, suggested to the Iraqi government that they might close the Italian embassy, even though, technically, Britain would not be at war with Italy until the following June. The Axis 'Pact of Steel' between Germany and Italy made their presence undesirable. The Colonels objected and the pro-British prime minister of the time was persuaded to push back, for one very good reason - secret lines of communication were being opened up between the Arab Committee and Berlin, and these depended on the go-between of the Italian ambassador.

As 1939 turned into 1940, the Red Fox wasted no opportunity to agitate on behalf of the Palestinians, as well as scheme against the Iraqi prime minister and what remained of pro-British elements in the Iraqi government. Finally, in March 1940, he and the Colonels forced the prime minister to resign and persuaded the Regent to appoint Rashid Ali as prime minister.

So this was the situation in the summer and autumn of 1940: a deteriorating situation in Europe after the lightning victory of Germany in France and the withdrawal of the British from Dunkirk; the general view across Iraq that Britain would soon be defeated, and that an accommodation should be made with Germany; and a new virulently anti-British Iraqi government led by Rashid Ali under the sway of the Red Fox and the Colonels. It was not an attractive picture that faced the British.

In June 1940, an assessment of the situation in Iraq by the Chiefs of Staff Committee in London concluded:

"The adherence to the cause of the Allies by Iraq is in considerable danger. Anti-British feeling runs high, especially among the younger army officers . . . German exploits do more than merely evoke admiration." [6]

At the same time, the Foreign Secretary, Lord Halifax, told the War Cabinet: *"The Arabs have largely lost confidence in the Allies to protect them and above all wish to be on the winning side."* [7]

Finally, when Italy declared war on Britain, ambassador Newton once again asked the Iraqis to close the Italian embassy. Again the British were rebuffed.

London was by now becoming alarmed. With the French out of the war, it was for a while unclear what would happen in Syria, which was still under direct rule from Paris. Would it follow the Vichy government, or declare for the new Free French movement under de Gaulle? By the end of June, it had declared for the Vichy Government, and a worrying new element had been introduced into the delicate balance of power in the Middle East. The following month, a plan was drawn up to ship an Indian brigade to Basra to shore up Britain's military presence, but at the last minute Ambassador Newton baulked. He was worried about upsetting Rashid Ali, who might see it as a hostile move. It was a decision that was to be rued nine months later. In August it was diverted to Suez, where Wavell had a more pressing need.

So when in January 1941, just as trainee Pilot Officer Dunford Wood arrived in Habbaniya, the British finally decided to move against Rashid Ali, they were woefully under prepared. Still, Newton was confident, and had no reason to think that he could not engineer the situation in a way that had worked so well in the past, and, emboldened by Wavell's successes in North Africa, the Regent was persuaded to ask Rashid Ali to resign.

At first Rashid Ali refused to go. This would have been unheard of when Feisal was King, and caused an uproar in the Iraqi Parliament, where some semblance of constitutional nicety still existed in the acceptance of a hierarchy headed by the Monarchy; even in the guise of the pro-British Regent.

Finally, in early February, Rashid Ali was forced to give way, though this was to prove just a tactical retreat. The Regent's pick to replace him, on the advice of the British, was a man called Taha al-Hashimi, who had previously been his minister of defence.[8] But at this juncture the British - through Al-Hashimi and the Regent - overplayed their hand. When Al-Hashimi attempted to order the four Colonels to new postings far from Baghdad, the officers refused. On 28th February, losing confidence in the situation and determined to act, they met in secret with the Red Fox and the ousted Rashid Ali to draw up plans for seizing back the initiative. They were also encouraged by more positive noises, finally, from Germany, after a recent propaganda trip that had been made to Syria and Lebanon by a German representative called Von Hentig. Reports had come back to the Red Fox from his agents in the region that the man had made quite an impression, organising film shows of Nazi military successes and anti-British lectures, and that at last it looked as though the Germans were beginning to take the Arabs seriously.[9] The stage was set; the storm was coming.

~

1. Freya Stark was to write later about the 'hands-off' approach to Iraq taken by the British: *"The important thing to notice is that—to a British view—the Arab world is a region of transit ... there is no British interest in Arabia as such; but it is a vital region from the fact that it lies between Asia and the Mediterranean, right across the highways of the Empire."* East is West, Freya Stark xix.

2. As the British ambassador reported just days after Feisal's death: *"It was King Feisal's skill and political subtlety which enabled him to hold the delicate balance between Sunni and Shia, and through his profound understanding of the Arab mind he was able to deal with his turbulent tribal chieftains with a marked degree of success."* *The National Archives* FO 371/16924, British ambassador, Sept 1933.

3. As the British Ambassador was to say a few years later: *"The British have created an impossible situation for themselves in the Middle East with their Zionist project*

in Palestine...Why would anyone in the region welcome the implanting of a colony of European Jews in the midst of over a million Christian and Muslim Palestinians?" Persian Gulf Command, Ashley Jackson.

4. From the British point of view the new Regent was in the same mould as Feisal, 'more English than the English', a man who would rather spend his time in Bond Street than any longer than was necessary in Baghdad. And who could blame him? As Anthony Eden, the British Foreign Secretary, observed with unconscious irony, *"while he is not a very strong character, there can be no question of his loyalty"*. The Role of the Military in Politics, Tarbush, p. 159.

5. Freya Stark, the British writer, traveller and SIS intelligence officer who was at the time working to bolster Britain's image in Iraq as the second secretary in the British Embassy in Baghdad, described him as a *"short, cautious and rather delicate looking man with red hair, blue eyes and a lisp...wearing his turban like a halo, with a sort of radiance, as of a just-fallen Lucifer."*

6. The National Archives, CAB 66/8/35.

7. The National Archives, CAB 67/6/49.

8. Al-Hashimi was a clever choice, as of all the Iraqi politicians, as a former Chief of the General Staff and Minister of Defence, he commanded the respect of the Iraqi army.

9. What had changed? The answer was Ribbentrop. Up until this point the German Foreign Minister had stuck slavishly to Hitler's line, and refused to get involved with the Arab question. However, in January 1941 some disturbing news was reaching him of an ambitious new plan of the Fuhrer's. It was one he didn't agree with. His thinking was, if he could light a fuse under the Middle Eastern tinderbox, perhaps Hitler's new plan would become redundant.

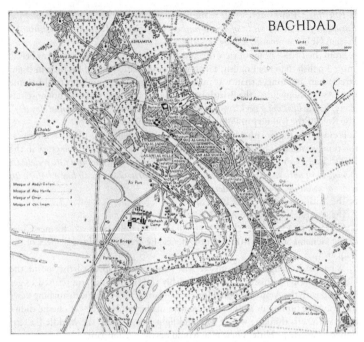

*1941 map of Baghdad showing the road to
Habbaniya to the west/left.*

Baghdad Coup

"The main street is like an English country town - thronged with chaps from all over the Near and Middle East... There are the Kurds, tall fellows with weather beaten faces in shaggy sheepskins who swagger around as if they own the place; Arabs from the south in their traditional woollen (at this time of year) robes, in browns and oranges, shifty and suspicious; haggling tribesmen from the Euphrates who hang around the bazaar, luring you in to sell you a copper teapot or a carpet; Indians in dhotis, Baluchis in woollen hats, and then the mullahs and the rabbis - there is a large Jewish community here, very wealthy by all accounts. That's before you count all the British officers on leave. Above it all strolls a class of man they call 'effendis', in fezzes or European suits, educated Baghdadis who run everything. All speaking in Arabic, Hindi, Persian, French, Armenian and God knows what, alongside a constant din, calls to prayer, camels, beggars, and donkeys. The only characters missing are the elephants of Delhi."[1]

ON APRIL 1ST THIS BAGHDAD din went suddenly quiet. Soldiers appeared on guard outside the radio station, the telephone exchange and the city's Post Offices, *'in a bored way... holding their bayonets as if they were fans,'[2]* and armoured cars stationed themselves on street corners at the main intersections. The newspapers said little, except that the Police Garden Party would be postponed. The bazaar emptied, windows were shuttered, and citizens stayed indoors. Army officers, according to Freya Stark accompanied by *'four doctors and a certificate of death by heart failure already written out',* went to the Palace in search of the Regent, but he had been forewarned and had already fled to the house of an aunt. The next morning, 2nd April, he appeared at the American Embassy asking for sanctuary. US Ambassador Knabenshue recounts what happened next:

> *"This morning at 8.45 the Regent came to me in native woman's dress covering dressing gown and pajamas to seek refuge in Legation, having been forewarned of attempt by four army colonels to force resignation of Prime Minister and reinstatement of Rashid Ali as Prime Minister...*
>
> *In consequence of consultation at Legation between the Regent, the British Ambassador and myself, I took Regent, accompanied by my wife as camouflage, to the British air base at Habbaniya in my car, with the Regent lying on the floor at the back covered by a rug."[3]*

As the Ambassador's Irish wife drily remarked afterwards, it was the only time she had had royalty at her feet.

Fortunately, a new British ambassador, Sir Kinahan Cornwallis, formerly an advisor to King Feisal, was due to arrive at Habbaniya that day by flying boat from Cairo, to replace Sir Basil Newton, and Knabenshue had been planning to drive down to greet him anyway. On arrival, the Regent emerged from the car in black pyjamas, clutching a revolver, to everyone's astonishment.[4] After recuperating from the harrowing ordeal, and after a debrief with Cornwallis, the Regent was flown on to Basrah and the safety of a British gunboat, and from there he was taken to Transjordan. As Dunford Wood recorded in his diary a few days later:

> *"Alarms and excursions. A few days ago the Regent was smuggled out of the country, the Prime Minister resigned, and the Army took over, one of the generals endeavouring to form a cabinet. Then occurs the most colossal flap. He is supposed to be anti-British, so the planes are bombed up, arms and ammunition dished out, everyone made to wear uniform and walk about armed, and no one allowed outside the camp. Yesterday an Iraqi aeroplane arrived, did three circuits and landed. The Gladiators were unable to get up to shoot him down, as they had been ordered to ring up the AOC before they took off, and his telephone was engaged. Chaps rush out to arrest the pilot, who says he has merely come for a meteorological exam, and he's right too!"*[5]

It had all come to a head during the previous two weeks. In early March the Iraqi Foreign Minister had been summoned to Cairo to meet Anthony Eden, who had remained there to try to sort out the Greek problem. Once again the Iraqi government was asked to sever diplomatic relations with the Italians, which, regardless of the Iraqi obligation under the 1930 Treaty, was now seen as a test of loyalty by the British. Back in Baghdad, Al-Hashimi realised that in the absence of support for such a move from the Red Fox and the Colonels, they would need to be neutralised. On 21st March the Foreign Office recorded a conversation between the Regent and Sir Basil Newton, in which the Regent told the ambassador of his plans with Al-Hashimi to remove the Colonels from office. Newton advised against it, on the basis that it might arouse a *"violent reaction, not only from the military clique, Mufti and Rashid Ali, but perhaps also from other elements, and the crisis may even involve our own military situation. We have therefore some misgivings about bringing the situation to a head at this moment.*[6]

This echoed Newton's pusillanimous attitude of the previous summer when considering whether to send an Indian Brigade to Basrah. He may also have had his own situation in mind, as he was due to be replaced within two weeks and return to London, and doubtless did not want any disturbance to upset his plans.[7]

However, nine days later the Regent ignored this advice and attempted to transfer one of the Colonels, Kamil Shabib, commander of the 1st Infantry Division, to Diwaniya, a tribal area 130 miles south of Baghdad on the road to Basrah. The order was rejected by his fellow Colonels, egged on by the Red Fox, and they finally decided to act, choosing 31st March, the final day of the closing session of parliament when all the politicians would be in town. Their first step was to extract, under threat, a letter of resignation from Al-Hashimi, before going in search of the Regent to ratify it.

The Regent's escape, however, left them in a dilemma. Without Royal approval, the resignation of Al-Hashimi and the appointment in his place of Rashid Ali was unconstitutional, and if the British had taught the Iraqis anything, the appearance at least of constitutional legitimacy was important. So after some confusion, on 3rd April Rashid Ali declared, over the radio, the formation of a 'Government of National Defence' with a new civilian cabinet, and issued two proclamations - the first accusing the Regent of treason, and the second pledging to 'carry on Iraq's national mission, to honour Iraq's international obligations, including the Anglo-Iraqi Treaty, and to keep Iraq out of the war.'[8]

This was a clear if disingenuous ploy to get the British to accept his new government, and to avoid precipitating them into any counter actions, given that the secret negotiations with Germany were still ongoing and had not yet reached a conclusion. Given the choice, Rashid Ali and the Colonels would have preferred not to move so early, but the Regent's actions had forced their hand.

Their job now was to avoid stirring up the British before they could secure help from Germany.

The arrival of Sir Kinahan Cornwallis, the new British ambassador, at this juncture was not coincidental. Back in London, the Foreign Office and the Chiefs of Staff Committee had already made the decision that they would need to move to protect their interests in the face of the rising tide of anti-British sentiment in the region. If their oil supplies or the land and air bridge between India and Egypt was interrupted, it would have serious consequences. In contrast to the man he was replacing, Cornwallis was a Middle East expert. He had been the Director of the Arab Bureau, a British intelligence unit, in Cairo in World War One, and then an advisor to the Iraqi Ministry of Interior and to King Feisal in the 1920s and early 30s, only being recalled after pressure from Rashid Ali in his first stint as prime minister on Feisal's death. So he and Rashid Ali had history. As Freya Stark suggested in her memoir 'East is West', if Cornwallis had been ambassador earlier, much of the subsequent trouble may have been avoided. Somerset de Chair, a British army captain who will loom large in the history of Habbaniya during the next few months, concurred - *"The Foreign Office had put the right man in the right place about five years too late."* [9] But in April 1941, he was exactly the right man for the crisis that was now unfolding.

His first act on landing in Habbaniya was to confer with the ousted Regent before he was whisked away to Basrah. His second was to delay recognising the new government, despite continuing professions of friendship from Rashid Ali, who went ahead and recalled Parliament to appoint a new Regent, Sharif Sharaf, a distant relative of the boy king. Ominously, the new Iraqi government was quickly recognised by Germany and Russia.

Moves were immediately put in train to bolster Britain's military forces in Iraq. On the 3rd, the War Office asked Wavell what forces he could spare to send to Iraq, despite the fact that just a month earlier it had been transferred from his Command to India's, given all the other pressures he was facing. He replied that

61

he would look at what he had available in Palestine, but he was not optimistic. On 6th April Habbaniya's commander, Air Vice-Marshal Smart, unsettled by the Iraqi moves to prevent British military personnel moving between Habbaniya and Baghdad, cabled the AOC Middle East in Cairo, Air Chief Marshal Longmore, for air reinforcements. Nothing, he was told, could be spared. All spare capacity had been sent to Greece and anyway, didn't Habbaniya have 84 planes of their own at their disposal?

That first week in April 1941 was perhaps the darkest period of the war for the British since Dunkirk, and the 6th was the darkest day of all. Benghazi fell to Rommel's forces on the 3rd, and Wavell realised that Tobruk would be next. With Tobruk in his hands, Rommel would be able to supply his forces for a final push on Cairo. With the switch of focus to Greece, the forces he had left to confront Rommel with were both under-resourced, and far too weak. It would not take much for the Germans to break through.

In Greece things looked just as unpromising, and Churchill was beginning to lose his nerve. But it was too late, as a British expeditionary force was already in position alongside the Greeks. Foreign Secretary Anthony Eden's attempts to get the Yugoslavs to come in on the side of the Allies had failed, and Prince Paul of Yugoslavia had signed an agreement with Hitler on 25th March.[10]

So Smart's plea on the 6th April came at the worst possible time. At dawn, the Germans crossed the Greek frontier, and Belgrade was bombed by Stukas. Thousands of civilians were killed, and the port of Piraeus was destroyed. That evening Generals Neame and O'Connor were captured by a German motorcycle patrol in the desert. Beset by these cascading problems, the last thing Wavell could focus on was Iraq, and on the 7th he cabled London to say that he could no longer spare any forces from Palestine, advising that help should be sent from India, as had been agreed with the War Office in the switch of Commands in early March. The situation on all fronts was critical. Moreover, he strongly advised that a political solution should be sought.

This lack of cooperation incensed Churchill. Auchinleck, C-in-C in India, was much more helpful. Fortunately (both for Iraq and the unit itself, considering what happened to Singapore nine months later), an infantry brigade was just then about to embark in India for Malaya. They were ordered to divert, and the ship left Karachi on the 12th bound for Basrah instead.[11]

However, as Smart well knew, reinforcements being sent to Basrah was a very different proposition to troops and planes for Habbaniya itself. Basrah was 370 miles to the south, the other side of Baghdad. His station was out on its own in the desert, highly vulnerable to attack. The omens did not look good. In addition to the restriction of movement being imposed on his personnel by the Iraqis, on the 5th April the British intercepted radio messages between the Italian embassy and the foreign ministry in Rome, through which an undertaking was issued to the Red Fox from Ernst von Weizsäcker, the minister of state in the German foreign ministry, in response to an earlier letter from the Iraqis asking for help, guaranteeing German support via Syria for any anti-British action they undertook 'as far as possible.'[12]

Smart was oblivious to this intercept. However, he was made privy to some other worrying intelligence from Ultra intercepts at Bletchley Park, that Germany's XI. Fliegerkorps - their paratrooper division - was being made ready for action, alongside a significant build-up of JU52 transport planes in the Balkans. Their purpose was unknown, and the British feared that they were being readied for Syria or Iraq. Smart was told to be prepared for an airborne attack on his camp.[13]

On the 4th, Smart had issued his first operational instruction to senior commanders to start preparing the base for combat, ordering the stepping up of patrols. In addition, tree pruning was begun to remove obstructions to the line of fire, and ammunition was issued. On the 7th, he gathered his senior commanders together to discuss next steps, and the initial instruction became 'Iraq Command Operation Order No 1':

"There is no question at present of intervention by Great Britain in what is, for the time being, a matter of internal Iraqi policy. There is, however, the possibility that the Iraqi Army may be encouraged by pro-Axis agitators to take some form of anti-British action, which may lead to attacks on RAF Cantonments."

As the only British ground forces in the camp, the No. 1 RAF Armoured Car Company was directed to set up an observation post on the escarpment on the Fallujah-Baghdad road, and on another one to the west of the base. They were to look out for airborne troops as well as Iraqi aircraft, and were issued with SOS Very light flares for raising the alarm. Everyone knew, though, that this unit would not stand much of a chance against a determined Iraqi advance. It consisted of eighteen World War One vintage Rolls-Royce armoured cars organised into three sections of six plus an HQ, with twelve officers and 160 men. In addition, they had two Vickers Dragon mark 1 artillery tractors, named HMT Walrus and HMT Seal, one of which had been converted into a tank by the Royal Ordnance factory in Woolwich with the addition of a turret taken from a Rolls Royce armoured car, the other into an armoured personnel carrier. They were very slow, and had not been in use for some years. Dusted down and re-crewed, they were now positioned outside the main gate of the camp.[14]

Inside the camp, meanwhile, RAF other ranks were issued with rifles and fifty rounds, officers with revolvers and twelve rounds, and plans were drawn up for the formation of *'The Habbaniya Air Striking Force'* under the overall command of Group Captain Walter Savile, 4 SFTS's commanding officer. However, although training was to be continued, it was clear something more proactive had to be done.

On the 8th, Dunford Wood reported in his diary:

*'HMAC' Euphrates, one of RAF Habbaniya's 1915
vintage Rolls-Royce armoured cars.*

> "Today a colossal formation is organised over Fallujah
> and Ramadi, but there is so much low-lying cloud that
> it is postponed. The German news says we are prisoners
> of war and that Italian transports have arrived in
> Basrah to take us away! And that the Iraqis have shot
> down some 18 British planes!" [15]

The 'colossal formation' finally took place on the 9th. As a
way to impress the Iraqis, it was very much a 1920s sabre-rattling
exercise that had been designed to scare tribesmen. However, the
flying school pulled it together, bolstered with some rusty pilots
from Headquarters staff:

> "We do a formation flight of four squadrons –
> Harts with Oxfords circling overhead and the three
> Gladiators down below. I went in Dan Cremin's front
> seat and we went over Fallujah and Ramadi." [16]

Another participant remembers it slightly differently. Squadron Leader Dudgeon had arrived at Habbaniya on 3rd April for a deserved rest. As the commander of 55 Squadron in North Africa, he had flown Blenheim bombers on over fifty missions against the Italians in just three months, and had recently been awarded the DFC. He soon realised that this would not be the rest he had been promised, vividly recalling this 'Demonstration flight' in his book 'The War that Never Was':[17]

> "48 pilots we managed to find, and so 48 aircraft flew. All instructors flew of course, plus a few of the more advanced pupils, and a couple of Greek pilots. Several different types were chosen – 32 Harts and Audaxes, 13 twin engined Oxfords and the three Gladiator biplane-fighters. Those out-of-date fighters, of course, were not flown by fighter pilots. They were only based (at Habbaniya) because they had been superannuated from the Western Desert theatre as being beyond practical use in a fighting role. They were kept as a sort of flying sports-car for Headquarters officers to use for any local travelling.
>
> This great gaggle – it deserved no better word – took to the air. As may be imagined from the comparatively unpractised rag, tag and bobtail in the pilot's seats, the quality of the formation itself was terrible. There were five flights in all. One each of Oxfords and Harts, and two of Audaxes, all cruising at the same speed and, God willing, in the same direction. The three fighters, flying faster, had a roving commission and swooped around, above and below the main formation. Fortunately, no aircraft came into collision. The whole of this lot traipsed back and forth near two local villages called Ramadi and Fallujah."

A Hart trainer taking part in the 'Demonstration Flight'
of 9th April 1941.

Following this exercise, *Operation Order No. 2* [18] set up a daily recce rota of aircraft, including one at night, to report movements on the Baghdad-Fallujah Road and the Habbaniya-Ramadi road. They were instructed not to fly below 1,000ft, nor to provoke the Iraqis or carry any bombs, and only to fire in self defence. The three Gladiators and six Audaxes were to stand by at half an hour notice for fighter duties, while twelve further Audaxes and fifteen Gordons were to be prepared as bombers at two hours readiness, as was a Valentia from the Communications flight, which was to have eight 250 lb bombs or four 500 lb bombs fused and prepared for loading on to the aircraft.[19] Greek pupil pilots from the Royal Hellenic Air Force were to be allowed to volunteer.

Finally, to complete the preparations, a partial blackout test was carried out.[20]

Meanwhile, the British convoy (BP7) was steaming towards Basrah, and was due to arrive on the 18th April. On board were an infantry brigade (the 20th) of the 10th Indian Division and a field regiment of artillery, under the command of Major General William Fraser. His orders were straightforward:

- *To occupy the Basrah-Shaibah area in order to ensure the safe disembarkation of further reinforcements and to enable a base to be established in that area.*

- *In view of the uncertain attitude of the Iraqi Army and local authorities, to face the possibility that attempts might be made to oppose disembarkation.*

- *Should the disembarkation be opposed, to overcome the enemy by force and occupy suitable defensive positions ashore as quickly as possible.*

- *To take the greatest care not to infringe the neutrality of Iran.*

It had, however, been packed for a non-operational landing - that's to say all the heavy equipment and vehicles were not prepared for immediate action or an opposed landing, as the ship had been loaded for arrival in Malaya before diversion to Iraq. Given the noises emanating from the Iraqi government, and the fact that they had a division stationed in Basrah, nothing could be taken for granted. On the other hand, Britain had every right under the Anglo-Iraqi Treaty to transit forces through the country, provided the Iraqi government was informed.

Cornwallis played his hand skillfully. Initially the plan had been to land the force without informing the Iraqis, but Cornwallis counselled the Foreign Office that this would only give the Iraqis an excuse to rise up against the British on the pretext of invasion. Moreover, Rashid Ali was still professing friendship, maintaining that nothing had changed, and claiming that he intended to carry on honouring the 1930 Anglo-Iraqi Treaty. In that case, reasoned

Cornwallis, here was an opportunity to test that sentiment, since the transition of British troops through Iraq was expressly provided for in the Treaty.

So the new ambassador waited until the 16th to inform Rashid Ali that British troops would be arriving the next day, as per her Treaty rights, hence giving the Iraqis no time to organise any resistance, should they be so minded. He intimated they were coming in order to open up the desert route to reinforce North Africa, and to sweeten the deal, suggested that if Rashid Ali cooperated, then the British would open informal relations with his new government. The Iraqi cabinet met on the 17th to consider the request and Rashid Ali, still keen to gain British recognition of his government, persuaded them to agree.

The same day, an advance party of the 20th Indian Brigade, a detachment of the 1st Battalion of the King's Own, were due to arrive in Basrah by air from Karachi, transported over four days and 1300 miles via Oman and Bahrain in fourteen transport aircraft in what was the world's first military airlift. They arrived in two waves, on the 17th, and the 24th, with the intention to then airlift them on to Habbaniya.

Rashid Ali tried to keep the agreement quiet, and there was nothing on the radio or in the Iraqi press about the troops arrival, so he was embarrassed when the BBC broadcast news of the landings being given a friendly reception in Basrah. The Red Fox and the Colonels were furious with the way he had, as they saw it, caved in, and now demanded that he lay down conditions: that the troops should transit through the country as soon as possible; no further troops should be landed until these had left; and that the strength of any troops landed should at no time exceed a brigade, or 3,000 men. Cornwallis cabled these new conditions to London but was instructed to ignore them. Strictly speaking, according to the Treaty, in time of war the British were entitled to move as many troops as they liked, and the Iraqis were obliged to provide all and any assistance that might be requested. However, Cornwallis was ordered not to make agreements with an Iraqi government which the British did not recognise, and to avoid 'entangling himself with explanations'.

Rashid Ali began to realise that he was now in a race against time to prevent the British moving against him. The next day he met the Italian ambassador, Luigi Gabrielli, and once again implored that support be sent by Germany as soon as possible, both in the form of arms from Vichy French Syria, and aircraft, to honour the letter that they had sent just a week before. He also offered the Axis powers the use of all Iraq's airfields, including Habbaniya.

However, back in Berlin things were still moving very slowly. Just as Wavell was preoccupied with Rommel's advances and Greek retreats - Rommel reached the Egyptian border in mid April, and British forces were already starting to plan for an evacuation from Greece - so the Germans had their hands full with the Greek offensive and preparations for Operation Barbarossa, which was shortly to be unleashed against Russia. However, there was one man in the German leadership who presciently believed that Barbarossa - scheduled to start at the beginning of June - was a colossal mistake.

Foreign Minister Joachim von Ribbentrop had been pressing for an alternative strategy against the British in the Middle East since the beginning of the year. In his view, it was a much more manageable prospect than a march on Moscow, and one that was guaranteed to bring the British to their knees without having to put one German foot on British soil.[21] Now, following Rashid Ali's coup, he decided to accelerate matters. On the 9th he met with Ernst Woermann, Head of the Political Department of the Foreign Ministry, to gain his support with Hitler. Woermann noted, *"there is now a cabinet (in Iraq) that was to be considered the most nationalist and pro-Axis this far, and according to reports has the full support of the Iraqi army".*[22]

As a result of this meeting, and with Woermann's agreement, Von Ribbentrop instructed the army to 'organise an intelligence service in the Middle East, which would have to be confined to purely military matters,' in addition to developing 'sabotage' and 'insurrections' in Palestine, Transjordan, and Iraq. The next day he asked for Hitler's approval for the dispatch of arms to the Iraqi rebels.

However, by the time of Rashid Ali's plea to the Italian ambassador, nothing further had happened. Hitler was preoccupied. A message came back to the German foreign ministry from the Italians, to the effect that *the Iraqi government was quite annoyed because it had yet received no reply to its request for Axis support by Axis aviation*" and that "*the situation was becoming downright critical.*"[23]

So on the 21st April, Von Ribbentrop again messaged Hitler, pointing out that support would have to come in by air, via Syrian landing grounds, and the agreement of the Vichy Government would be required. Three days later he finally got Hitler's attention by skilfully pointing out that any defeat of the Iraqis by the British could have an adverse effect on Turkey's attitude to Germany, and Hitler depended on a friendly Turkey to protect the southern flank of his proposed operation against Russia.

Finally, on the 25th, Rashid Ali concluded an agreement with the Italian ambassador, under which the Axis powers agreed to supply financial and military aid to the Iraqi government for war against Britain. It also provided for the future union of Iraq and Syria, for long a dream of the Red Fox and all Arab nationalists, as well as oil concessions and the use of ports and airports for the Axis powers.[24]

So after two weeks of waiting and just a day after Von Ribbentrop finally learned of the launch date of Barbarossa in June, Hitler approved his request to ship arms to Iraq. But he was still cautious. Surely, given the reports that 14,000 British troops had disembarked at Basrah, with a further 14,000 on the way, was it not too late? In reply, Von Ribbentrop, determined that Hitler should not backtrack, pointed out that *"English sources were spreading propaganda figures that have no relation to the facts."*

He also reminded the Fuhrer what a detrimental impact continuing passage of Indian troops through Iraq could have on Rommel's North Africa campaign, pointing out that this was a golden opportunity to strike at Britain when their defence of the Suez Canal was relatively weak.

At this juncture, then, there were four key actors who could have an influence on how the Iraq situation developed, but only two of them recognised its strategic importance. Wavell and Hitler were preoccupied with what they saw as bigger issues, while only Churchill and Von Ribbentrop saw the danger and the opportunity. If roles had been reversed, things might have turned out very differently.

Nevertheless, even at this moment, the situation favoured the Iraqis. Reinforcements landing in Basrah would take weeks to have an effect, given the distance they were from Baghdad and Habbaniya, and the fact that all the Iraqis needed to do was breach the Tigris and Euphrates flood defences to make their progress north painfully slow. Wavell's refusal - or inability - to send help from Egypt meant that Habbaniya would need to cope on its own. But how could it possibly survive, with only a flying training school and just thirty-five trained flying instructors, in an assortment of obsolete training aircraft, against a professional Iraqi army and a British trained air force?

~

1. Colin Dunford Wood, private papers.
2. East in West, Freya Stark, p140.
3. Quoted in Ashley Jackson, Persian Gulf Command, from FRUS, Knabenshue to Secretary of State, 2-4-41, p166.
4. An episode well told in Memoirs of a Diplomat's Wife by Betty Holman, the wife of the Counsellor in Baghdad.
5. The War Diaries of Colin Dunford Wood, Vol 1, 8th April 1941.
6. The National Archives, FO 371/27062 - 24 March 1941.

7. The Foreign Office had finally decided they needed someone else in post, who had more experience of dealing with the Iraqis, but it was taking them a while to get him out there.

8. The National Archives FO 371/77076.

9. The Golden Carpet, Somerset de Chair, p122.

10. The Yugoslavs themselves were appalled, and deposed Prince Paul two days later in a coup, but the instability played right into Hitler's hands. As Wavell wrote at the time in a message marked Most Secret and Very Personal: The Jug (with apologies to Lewis Carroll): *"I sent a message to the Jug, I told him not to be a mug. I said he must be badly cracked, To think of joining Hitler's pact. The Jug replied: 'But don't you see, How difficult it is for me...'"* Wavell, Victoria Schofield, p181.

11. There were already contingency plans in place to reinforce the Persian Gulf from India to protect the Iranian and Iraqi oil fields in the face of Russian aggression from the north - codenamed Operation Sabine - so these were quickly dusted down. This brigade was to be the advance guard of a planned force of three divisions.

12. Iraq 1941, Robert Lyman, p 28.

13. In the event they were dropped on Crete in May.

14. The Armoured Car Company had been introduced into Iraq in late 1922 when the RAF had taken over responsibility for maintaining order from the British Army. In normal times, its role, in addition to airfield defence, had been wide-ranging - to aid the civilian authorities in securing the borders and controlling the tribes, attending to aircraft breakdowns, and, from the 1930s, protecting the oil pipelines running between Kirkuk, Haifa and Tripoli, as well as running ration convoys to the Levies that guarded them. Occasionally too, they were required to escort various dignitaries around the country. In carrying out these multiple tasks they were used to roaming far and wide across deserts and mountains, and it took a resourceful individual to be able to manage the harsh conditions, where wireless communications were patchy, water scarce, and navigation often only possible by the stars. This bred a special close-knit culture and independent spirit amongst the armoured car crews, which harked back to the free-roaming Yeomanry Desert Patrols formed in the Western desert in 1916. They had been resurrected, famously, as the Long Range Desert Patrols in Egypt the previous year, a forerunner of the SAS.

15. The War Diaries of Colin Dunford Wood, Vol 1, 8th April 1941. The comment about the German news report is significant - evidently action was expected at any minute, even though the official line at that stage, just a week after the coup, was that it was an 'internal matter' that was unlikely to spill over into conflict.

16. The War Diaries of Colin Dunford Wood, Vol 1, 11th April 1941.

17. Dudgeon also had experience of flying Audaxes against tribesmen in the North West Frontier in the late 1930s, so of all of the airmen at Habbaniya in April 1941, he was by far the most battle hardened and experienced.

18. The National Archives, AIR 23:5924.

19. Communication Flight in Combat - RAF in Iraq 1941, Michael Skeet.

20. The record states that it was 'mostly successful', though it was noted that the HQ officers' mess and officers' club made little or no attempt to comply.

21. Ribbentrop was not alone in being nervous of the plans for Barbarossa. There is a curious postscript to this story. A few weeks later, on 10th May, Rudolf Hess parachuted into Scotland with secret peace terms, almost certainly without Hitler's authority. It was an attempt to make peace with Britain before Barbarossa kicked off, as he knew that opening a second front against Russia would be a huge risk with the first front still raging. It was telling that the only condition Hess made relating to affairs outside the European theatre concerned Iraq: Britain had to agree to withdraw. He knew that without access to oil, Britain's forces in the Middle East would be neutered.

22. Documents on German Foreign Policy, 1918–1945, from the Archives of the German Foreign Ministry (DGFP): Vol X11, no. 299.

23. DGFP, vol. XII, no. 401.

24. Persian Gulf Command, Ashley Jackson, p181.

*Squadron Leader A.G. 'Tony' Dudgeon with his dachshund
'Frankie', Habbaniya, May 1941.*

The Maverick

ONE MAN WHO UNDERSTOOD what this meant was Squadron
Leader Dudgeon. An old Etonian and a natural rebel against
authority, Dudgeon found the complacency of the senior officers
of the flying school disturbing. As he described himself in his book
'Hidden Victory', his philosophy was 'Results first; rules second.'[1]
His arrival at Habbaniya for 'rest and recuperation' at this critical
juncture was to prove crucial, and was the first of three key factors
that would decide the coming battle.

Within days, on April 3rd, he got together with his boss, the
Chief Flying Instructor, Wing Commander Ling, to figure out
what could be done to prepare the camp for war.

The first thing to work out was how many planes they could get in the air. On paper the official establishment, as Air Marshal Longmore had pointed out when Smart had asked for reinforcements, was eighty-four airframes.

The 'Demonstration flight' was an eye opener. First of all, many of the planes were not airworthy, and second, the pilots were inexperienced. The most they could muster were thirty-five flying instructors, many of whom had had no operational experience, while of those who had, the majority had been posted to 4 SFTS as 'unsuitable' for operations. The remainder were ex-operational pilots like Dudgeon himself, ordered to Habbaniya for a rest after a long spell of action. Then there were the pupils, only four of whom were qualified to fly, the others either still training or flying as navigators.[2] Last, the vast majority of the planes they had were unarmed trainers.

Ling and Dudgeon quickly set to work figuring out how they could be armed. It looked daunting. The Hart trainers had had all their gun mountings, cables and bomb levers stripped out, in order to make them lighter for training and to give space for dual controls, so there was little that could be done with them. However the Audaxes appeared more promising. They already had machine guns, and were used for gunnery training, as well as two 'light series' bomb racks normally used for practice bombs.[3] Dudgeon knew from his experience of flying Hart bombers - on whose design an Audax was based - on the North West Frontier before the war that they were capable of carrying much larger bombs. But in order to carry the bigger 250 lb munitions they needed the correct bomb release gear, similar to those normally fitted to the seven obsolete Fairey Gordons biplane bombers the base used for towing targets for shooting practice. These were called universal bomb racks - one on each wing.

So Dudgeon and Ling went to see the school's commanding officer, Group Captain Savile, with a proposal to upgrade the racks. Savile, nicknamed the 'Butcher' by the pupils for his uncompromising bullheadedness, rejected the plan out of hand. With the time honoured reflex of the risk-averse middle manager he referred to the manual, pointing out that the maximum permitted bomb load of an Audax was four small 20 lb bombs. Ling pushed back, pointing out that the Audax was built on the same airframe as the Hart, which could carry much larger loads. An argument ensued, bordering on insubordination. Eventually Savile agreed to remit the decision to the engineering department.

However, like Savile, the engineers were unwilling to risk authorising the change, so a signal was sent to London. As Dudgeon remembers:

> "The engineers' message turned out to be one which still sticks in my mind as a classic of wooden-headedness. They were not going to risk being held in ridicule for proposing something out of the ordinary. They signalled the Air Ministry, asking blandly: 'What is the bomb-load on an Audax?'"

What the Air Ministry thought of the fatuous question was anybody's guess, since the manual clearly stated it was eight 20 lb bombs. The answer that came back was as expected. The engineers smugly turned down the request.

Dudgeon was exasperated. Clearly the flying school authorities were not in a war frame of mind. Having just returned from a very successful fifty mission campaign in Libya harassing the Italians, he was used to getting things done. It took innovation and daring to win wars, not rules and processes. So he persevered with his boss, Ling, explaining that when flying Harts on the North West Frontier they sometimes carried even more than the regulation 500 lb, smuggling tinned meat, sausages, kippers, whisky and on one occasion a movie projector up to Himalayan outposts - and at high altitude too. Ling agreed to ask Savile for permission to at least run a test. This time the Group Captain reluctantly agreed, so long it was solely on Dudgeon's responsibility.

The test was a success. A specially rigged Audax took off with two 250 lb bombs without a problem, and suddenly everyone was happy.

Next, they needed to find the bomb racks. There were thirty-eight suitable ones in the stores. They set to work adding fourteen of them back to the Fairey Gordons, and the rest to the Audaxes.

The Oxfords provided the final challenge. They normally carried a crew of three alongside training equipment, so weight here was not the problem. However, their bomb wells were designed to fit light 9 lb practise bombs, and when Dudgeon tried to fit 20 lb-ers he discovered that the tail fin of the 20 lb bombs was longer than the bomb well. Within days he designed a pair of metal plates that had the effect of lowering the end of the bomb rack, meaning that it projected an inch below the fuselage, clearing the obstruction.

So another message was sent to AHQ in London suggesting the modification, and asking for permission to test it, and again the response was bureaucratic. There was no knowing what would happen to the aerodynamics with the tail fins of 20 lb bombs sticking out, and there was a real danger of the bombs getting dislodged on landing or take off, causing a fatal crash.

By this time concerns were being raised amongst the senior commanders as to what this maverick Dudgeon was up to, and the AOC, Smart, got involved. A note was sent directly to Dudgeon's boss, Ling, ordering that the experiment be discontinued. Dudgeon describes mulling this over with Ling in the officer's mess bar, and their decision that Ling would not pass on this written order until Dudgeon had taken off on his test flight. To avoid blame falling on others, Dudgeon borrowed tools and secretly made two sets of plates himself. He then fitted a set to an Oxford, loaded the eight bombs and took off. Once again it went smoothly. Nothing more was said. By the time the planes were due to go into action, no one was going to argue any more..[4]

~

1. When, many years later, after the war, Dudgeon was asked to carry out a review of the terms and conditions under which airmen served, one sceptic expressed surprise, knowing Dudgeon's unconventional approach to authority. *"Why Dudgeon? He has always thrown Queen's Regulations out of the window."* To which the AOC replied, *"Then open the window."*

2. The Four Musketeers - Dunford Wood, Haig, Pringle and Gillespy were to have their Wings awarded on 16th April. Or rather three, because Gillespy failed his navigation exam - but that was overlooked when roles were allocated.

3. Lightweight metal brackets that were bolted under each wing which could carry four 20 lb bombs each, making a total payload of 160 lb. The War That Never Was, Tony Dudgeon, p 54.

4. The end result was fifty-nine serviceable, bombed-up aircraft: twenty-seven Oxfords, seven Gordons, twenty-two Audaxes and three Gladiators. The latter were short of ammunition belts, but pupils were put to work in relays to operate an antiquated belt making machine in the station armoury. It took about an hour to feed in nine hundred cartridges, which would last the four guns of a Gladiator around ten seconds. They worked round the clock, and soon the belts were piling up.

The Storm Approaches

On 14th April, regular flying training was suspended, to be substituted with an intensive course of ground instruction in bomb aiming and rear gunning. On the 17th Dunford Wood noted *"Aircraft dispersed everywhere, and all over the polo ground."* This was a wise precaution. In a message the previous week from the Baghdad embassy to Smart, the head of the military mission, General Waterhouse, had advised dispersing all aircraft at night.

The problem was that the main airfield was outside the main perimeter fence and in full view of the escarpment. Added to this, there were not enough hangers to house all the planes. So in mid April bulldozers had been set to work to make the polo ground and the golf course, which were adjacent to each other and on the other side of the camp and obscured by trees, landing ready. The bunkers were flattened to make space for additional dispersal grounds, and the planes were split between two main locations - the larger Oxfords in the hangars accessed from the main airfield via a gate in the perimeter fence, while the Audaxes were stationed on the now enlarged polo ground, with tents erected for pilots to sleep in when on night duty.

Help, too, started to arrive. On 16th April hundreds of boxes of leaflets turned up, printed in Cairo and Jerusalem and intended to be dropped over Baghdad to influence Iraqi public opinion; also six additional Gladiator fighters, which had been dug out of storage in Egypt. Unfortunately the ferry pilots who brought them - two Free French, a Pole, a Yugoslav and two RAF pilots - despite pleas from Smart, were not allowed to stay, and they were flown back to Cairo.[1]

Meanwhile, far to the south, the eight ship BP7 convoy was approaching the Shatt al Arab river, the confluence of the Tigris and Euphrates in the Persian Gulf, with the 20th Indian Infantry Brigade. On the east bank was Persia, and its oil terminal at Abadan forty miles upriver. On the west bank was Iraq, with Basrah a further forty miles upriver.[2]

The Brigade commander, Brigadier Powell, considered how best he would land his force. The problem was that he had no idea whether the landing would be opposed or not, and indeed his original orders had left open that very possibility. He had three options: to land at the mouth of the river, at Fao, and march upstream; to land in Kuwait, fifty miles to the west, and march the hundred miles inland to Basrah across the desert; or to sail right up the river to Basrah. In the end he chose the latter, as both of the other options would give the Iraqis plenty of forewarning, and in any case the fiction could be preserved that this was a harmless, business as usual exercise of Britain's treaty rights. Besides, just two days earlier Rashid Ali had raised no serious objections when informed, a fact that was communicated to the task force flagship by radio as it was approaching the coast.

The ships arrived in Basrah on the 18th and started to disembark. The dock area was secured by the 2/7 Gurkha Rifles, while the rest of the troops landed the following day. As it turned out, the landing went smoothly and most Iraqis in Basrah were friendly, although the dock labourers were uncooperative and went on strike, forcing the soldiers to unload the ships themselves.[3] Historically, the south of the country around Basrah had always been the most pro-British.

However, it wasn't long before the Iraqis revealed more of their hostile intentions. The day the first seaborne troops disembarked at Basrah, two Valentia transport aircraft began to ferry the advance guard - the King's Own - by air up to Habbaniya. They were instructed to land en route at the K3 pumping station at Haditha, the switch point of the Kirkuk-Haifa-Tripoli pipeline, where there were reports of Iraqi troops. The British were worried it was the prelude to a diversion of oil supplies being planned by the Iraqi Government. On landing, they were immediately attacked by Iraqi soldiers.[4] After a short skirmish, the crew and fifteen soldiers were taken prisoner, and the plane burned. The second aircraft tried to help but was shot up, and continued on to Habbaniya with two wounded crew.

In Basrah, the new Indian Brigade secured the port area, the civilian airfield, the power station, and the wireless transmitter, and set up a defensive perimeter around the RAF base at Shaibah. Their instructions were now to make Basrah ready for the arrival of the next convoy, due at the end of the month, which would bring the Brigade up to divisional strength. News quickly reached Baghdad, which reported that the British units were digging in and showed no signs of transiting, as had been stipulated by Rashid Ali. On the 21st Rashid Ali summoned Ambassador Cornwallis to protest, declaring it to be a breach of the Treaty, and forbidding the landing of any further troops. And in a clear attempt to ratchet up the pressure, he confirmed British suspicions by ordering the Iraqi Army to occupy the Kirkuk oil fields and cut the Haifa pipeline (flowing to British controlled Palestine), and in its place open up the Tripoli branch (going to Vichy controlled Syria) that had been closed since the defeat of France in 1940. The supply of oil that the Royal Navy's Mediterranean fleet relied on suddenly dried up.

For the British, this was a virtual declaration of war. On 28th Cornwallis was back, informing Rashid Ali that more troops would be landing imminently. This time the niceties were dispensed with, and the Iraqi prime minister declared that if they landed, it would be interpreted as an act of war. Moreover, he pointed out that the British troops seemed to be making a base in Basrah, which was in contravention to an amendment to the Treaty that had been made in July 1940, which stated that 'Army bases should not be established or troops stationed in Iraq'. Cornwallis, having only just arrived back in the country, had no knowledge of this amendment, and in fact quickly discovered that it had been unilaterally inserted by the previous Rashid Ali administration. He explained that they would disembark anyway, in accordance with Britain's ratified treaty rights. Further, he requested permission to evacuate British women and children from Baghdad. To that last request, Rashid Ali agreed.

So over the next twenty-four hours Cornwallis set in motion a plan called Operation Concentrate that he had already discussed with Knabenshue, the American ambassador. Thirty RAF buses and trucks, together with a 38-seater hired from a local bus company, were to arrive at a pick up point at Baghdad's civil airport on 29th, from where they would drive expatriate women and children out to Habbaniya, for onward transfer out of the country. The airlift was to be predominantly for British and American families, but other nationalities were encouraged to join if there was room. For those who stayed behind, the British and American embassies provided sanctuary.[5] As the evacuation began, Smart sent a worried signal to Cairo:

> *"Situation grave... Ambassador under impression Iraqi attitude is not bluff and may mean definite promise (of) Axis support. Unmistakable signs treaty may be repudiated."*[6]

He was already stepping up preparations. Around the time that the Valentias had been attacked on the pipeline, a new message had gone out from Habbaniya AHQ to all commanders:

> *"HMG have now decided to take a strong line of action which might well result in the present Iraqi Government adopting hostile measures against British interests in Iraq."*

The same day, AHQ asked the relevant commanders how many men 4 SFTS, the Supplies Depot, and the Communications flight could spare for ground defence. 4 SFTS offered sixty-five, including three officers, which were most of the ground crew and the bulk of the students; the Supplies depot, nil. And the Comms flight, one officer and ten men, though they explained that this offer would need to be withdrawn if any of the Valentias were required to go into action. Headquarters staff said they could provide one officer and thirty-five men.

The planes, meanwhile, were organised into two main wings under Ling and Dudgeon, under the overall command of Group Captain Savile.

Ling was to command the Audaxes, which would operate from the polo field. They were to be organised into two squadrons - 'A' and 'C'. Ling was to lead 'C' Squadron while Wing Commander Hawtrey was co-opted from the Headquarters staff to lead 'A' Squadron.[7]

The two squadrons totalled twenty-one Audaxes, eleven of which were equipped with eight of the smaller, 20 lb bombs, while ten were fitted with the 250 lb bombs with the new universal brackets. In total, they had twenty pilots to fly them, which included fifteen operational pilots - including two more Wing Commanders brought in from HQ, Glynn Silyn-Roberts and Paul Holder - and the recently graduated four Musketeers, who were initially given reconnaissance duties in 'C' Squadron under Ling's watchful eye.

Meanwhile Dudgeon was to command the twenty-seven Oxfords and seven Gordons - designated as 'B' Squadron - along with nine Gladiators, as 'D' Squadron, from the main airfield. Dudgeon led the Oxfords, while Flight Lieutenant Cleaver led the Gladiators and Flight Lieutenant Evans led the Gordons. Between them they could muster nineteen pilots.

Finally Flight Lieutenant Skeet commanded the three Valentias of the communications flight, which had been converted to bombers.

Training, however, was to be stepped up. The AOC apparently was keen to make up for lost time. Dunford Wood was already feeling the lack of flying practice over the past few weeks:

> *"So today I go to C squadron and do message-picking-up, with White as my first passenger. My flying is shocking since it's a month since I last flew solo, and I can hardly see the message poles. I miss first time and second time break a pole; then it's time for breakfast."* [8]

Despite the frantic preparations, camp life seemed to go on almost as normal during that last week of April. On the 27th Dunford Wood described a big party on the Saturday night in the Club with the newly arrived officers from the King's Own: *"A most enjoyable party, majority army, from which I escaped at about midnight"*. The next day he took his polo pony, Finjan, across the Bunds, after a lazy Sunday lunch at the Lake Hotel on Lake Habbaniya, as two flying boats bobbed on the water.

It was hard to believe that there was a war on, or that it would soon come to Habbaniya.

~

1. The original plan, proposed by the AOC-in-C in Cairo, Air Marshal Longmore, had been to send a squadron of Wellington bombers with the Gladiators, but this was vetoed by the Air Ministry in London, who considered that Habbaniya had quite enough aircraft of their own to deal with the situation. They clearly had little idea of the age and condition of these obsolete training aircraft.
2. As Harry Hopkins, an advisor to Roosevelt who had recently visited the area, famously quipped: 'The Persian Gulf is the arsehole of the world and Basra is eighty miles up it.'
3. Iraq 1941, Robert Lyman, p31.
4. Dust Clouds in the Middle East, Christopher Shores, p166 - Shores refers to K4 which never existed.
5. There was a fear that if hostilities broke out, feelings amongst the local population could get ugly - they had already been whipped up to fever pitch by the propaganda that had been fed through Nazi radio broadcasts and German owned newspapers, bolstered by Iraqi government propaganda since Rashid Ali's coup.

There was a lot to hang propaganda off - while it was mostly related to Palestine, and the way the British treated the Arabs and encouraged the Jews, or so it was alleged - it was also fuelled by the string of defeats that the British had suffered over the past month. As far as the Iraqis were concerned, Britain was finished. It was a view shared widely around the world in the Spring of 1941.

6. Wavell, John Connell, p 433.

7. Hawtrey was particularly useful, as he was officially the 'Inspector of the Royal Iraqi Air Force', so he knew their capabilities well.

8. The War Diaries of Colin Dunford Wood, Vol 1, 21st April 1941.

Part 2

Flap! Flap!

"30th April: Yesterday evening all British women and children were evacuated from Baghdad, and it is said that the Iraqis were about to resist a landing of further troops of the force already here. This morning the alarm goes at about 4am and we go down to the flights and prepare planes for war. An Iraqi officer comes in by car to the AOC and out again, presumably with some sort of ultimatum. Then troops and armoured cars appear on the Plateau and at 8am I go off with James Fairweather to reconnoitre them. I keep her at 1,000 ft and we see 3 guns, 9 or so AFVs and about one battalion of troops all lined up ready to fire at the camp. I then land her on the polo pitch and we report to AHQ. A shave and wash and some breakfast, and now what!?

Just done a two hour recce of the Plateau, Fallujah and Fallujah Plain in an Audax with Sgt Douglas, 13:30 to 15:30. What a time! Saw 18 horse drawn 18 pounders the other side of Fallujah Plain, and Bofors guns, howitzers and M/Gs on the Plateau. Simply grand at 500 feet and AOC very pleased with my report, and asks me to do a dawn patrol. I tell Ling and he says "Yes! Yes!" and details Haig for it according to his roster. Very tired..." [1]

THE FIRST NEWS HABBANIYA HAD of the approach of Iraqi troops was a phone call just after 03:00 from General Waterhouse in the Embassy in Baghdad. The duty staff had woken him with news of large numbers of Iraqi military vehicles crossing the King Feisal Bridge to the west bank of the Tigris. At first they feared for the embassy, which was just five hundred yards upstream. But the troops continued west, towards Habbaniya. Waterhouse sent a ciphered message to Habbaniya, and Smart called his commanders together just after 04:00, but not before having raised the General Alarm. This caused chaos around the camp, as no one knew what to do. In the meeting the defence plan was activated, and Ling's squadron put on standby to get Audaxes in the air at first light to recce the Plateau. Flight Sergeant Mornington Wentworth of the RAF Armoured Cars Company recalled what happened:

> "The Rolls Royce armoured car and wireless tender were called back into camp from the observation posts. The alarm went off and we were ordered to man the cars. They were in the bays and we sat there until daylight, and when we looked up on the top of the Plateau, there was the long line of the Iraqis, with huge guns, facing the camp...a nasty looking situation." [2]

In ordering their withdrawal, Smart clearly wanted to avoid an escalation of the conflict. At 06:00 an Iraqi officer in a staff car appeared at the main gates saying he had a message for the commander of the camp. The note he delivered was to the point:

> "For the purposes of training we have occupied the Habbaniya hills. Please make no flying or going out of any force or persons from the cantonment. If any aircraft or armoured car attempts to go out it will be shelled by our batteries, and we will not be responsible for it."

Smart had to think fast. He knew that he would need instructions on how to react from Whitehall, but it was 03:00 in London. So for now he sent back the following message:

> *"Any interference with training flights will be considered an 'act of war' and will be met by immediate counter-offensive action. We demand the withdrawal of the Iraqi forces from positions which are clearly hostile and must place my camp at their mercy."*

Having forwarded the two messages on to Cornwallis in Baghdad and the AOC in Cairo, along with a plea for air reinforcements to be sent forthwith and for Cornwallis to use his best offices to get the Iraqis to withdraw by nightfall, he met up with the camp commanders again at 07:00. Ling had already conducted the first recce of the day, having flown across the Plateau and over the lake, and estimated that about 2,000 troops had already arrived, with tanks, armoured cars, and artillery already in position and trained on the camp, just a few hundred yards from the edge of the airfield. Further trucks, tanks and towed artillery were streaming down the road from Fallujah, and he reckoned the full force would number a full division of 9,000 troops within twenty-four hours. Now the light was properly up, the Iraqis could clearly be seen on top of the 150ft escarpment from all around the camp.

With his ground commanders, Smart reviewed the defence scheme. To oppose the Iraqis on the ground, other than the armoured car company, there were six companies of Levies (mostly Assyrians, though including one Kurdish company), totalling 1,199 men and officers, and the 364 men of the King's Own who had been flown in from Basrah. The camp perimeter had been divided into three sectors, each covered by a company of Levies with the rest as a mobile reserve, with each block house containing two NCOs and six troopers. However, they were lightly armed, with only one machine gun unit with ancient Hotchkiss and Lewis guns, one mortar section, and one Boys anti-tank rifle. The King's Own were marginally better equipped, with a number of Vickers machine guns and several more anti-tank rifles. Half of them were set to guard the main camp installations such as the hospital, power station, water tower and fuel store, while the remainder joined the Levies reserve.

The armoured cars, with their heavy Vickers machine guns, were to be used both as part of the reserve and, if necessary, in a nighttime offensive capacity. Meanwhile, aircrew and spare depot staff were to be organised into the agreed squads, and distributed around the camp to dig slit trenches and prepare defensive positions.

These dispositions, however, were a headache for Savile and Ling. Nobody would know where anybody was anymore. If fighting began, it threatened to leave the pilots and their observer-gunners to re-arm and refuel the planes themselves, which meant that in the event of multiple sorties in the day, turnaround would slow to a crawl. It was just about doable for the pilots to prepare their own planes for the occasional recce flight, despite the sweltering heat, but not during a full scale battle.

So the Air Striking Force commanders insisted they were given a list of exactly where in the camp their men had been sent, so that in the event of action, they knew how to recall them. Before ground defence could be considered, the planes had to be made ready - they were, after all, Habbaniya's best hope of inflicting damage on the Iraqis.

And this was the most worrying aspect for Smart. The ground defence scheme looked well organised on paper, but it would not last an hour against the armour and artillery that the Iraqis had available. The camp had none - unless you counted the thin skinned armoured cars from the time of Lawrence and the two old converted artillery tractors. There were two ceremonial Great War howitzers which stood on the lawn of Air House, but they were too thickly covered in paint to be useable.

So if the Iraqis felt like it, they could literally walk into the camp. Their only hope of effective resistance were the planes. But clearly, once the Iraqis swarmed down the escarpment, their effectiveness would be limited, as they were only truly potent as an offensive weapon. The squadron commanders certainly realised this. As they dispersed back to their various stations to put the agreed arrangements in motion, Air Vice-Marshal Smart, a man who had not seen action for eighteen years, an instructor to the core, waited for instructions from London, Cairo, the embassy, on what to do.

At around 11:00, Ambassador Cornwallis replied. He advised Smart not to engage in offensive action until he had heard back from London. Then, half an hour later, the Iraqi envoy was back. He had a new message, to the effect that since the British had not respected the terms of the 1930 Treaty, the Iraqi commanding officer, Colonel Fahmi Said, would allow no further training until the terms were restored. Now at least Smart and Cornwallis knew who they were dealing with - Said was one of the four Colonels of the 'Golden Square' and commander of Iraq's most modern fighting force, the Independent Mechanised Brigade. As for not respecting the treaty, this referred to the disembarkation of the second tranche of troops of the 10th Indian Division at Basrah the day before, without Iraqi government permission.

§

From Rashid Ali's point of view, along with that of the Red Fox and the Colonels, the British had forced his hand. It was clear that the build up of British forces in Basrah would now continue, and that there was no intention to transit them through the country on the way to Palestine or Egypt. Although they had not yet received the help they had requested from Germany, the Iraqis felt they could wait no longer, and in any case, the outbreak of hostilities would likely accelerate help from the Axis powers. For the past few days, more urgent messages had been sent to Berlin and Rome via the Italian legation. This time Rashid Ali was more specific - he asked for captured British weapons held in Vichy controlled Syria with which the Iraqi army would be familiar, namely four hundred Boys armour piercing rifles, sixty armour piercing cannons, 10,000 hand grenades, six hundred Bren guns and eight four Vickers heavy machine guns, along with over 100,000 rounds of ammunition.[3]

In Berlin, Ribbentrop began organising ways to get the weapons to Iraq, having finally secured Hitler's tentative approval on the 26th. Key to this operation would be the cooperation of the Vichy government. As a first step he contacted Otto Abetz, the German ambassador in Paris, to sound out the French. He also put Fritz Grobba on standby to return to Baghdad at a moment's notice.

While they waited, the Iraqis were reasonably confident that they could prevent the breakout of the British troops in Basrah by breaching the Bunds and flooding the lower reaches of the Euphrates, which they did on the 29th. This effectively cut off Habbaniya from the east, and made an advance north from Basrah extremely difficult. What they could not prevent was the increased build up of airlifted reinforcements, which finally persuaded the Red Fox and the Colonels that the time had come to march on Habbaniya. Besides, they were supremely confident. Colonel Said was raring to show off what his Mechanised Brigade could do. The Royal Iraqi Air Force was also put on standby. This was, on paper, a formidable force. It boasted a total of 116 aircraft, of which about half were fully operational, including a squadron of Hawker Nisrs - similar to the Audax but with more powerful Bristol Pegasus radial engines, and known as "Peggy" Audaxes - a squadron of Gladiators, and, more menacingly, three bomber squadrons equipped by modern Italian monoplanes - Bredas and Savoias - and American Northrop fighter bombers. The three engined Savoias carried a 2,750 lb bomb load and a crew of five. The newer Northrops, fortuitously for the British, were unarmed, as they had been supplied that way by the Americans. Although armaments for them had been ordered by the Iraqi Air Force, the Royal Navy managed to divert the ship carrying these supplies from Basrah to Karachi on April 19th, and subsequently all sixteen of them were destroyed on the ground by British saboteurs.[4]

In Baghdad, meanwhile, the British Embassy was effectively under siege. The buses of evacuees had left at midday, shadowed by an RAF Oxford piloted by Wing Commander Paul Holder, and were now sharing the road, surreally, with an advance guard of Iraqis heading towards the Plateau. After the Iron Bridge in Fallujah they split - the Iraqis turning left, up to the Plateau, the evacuees continuing straight on to the gates of the camp. For many of them, it can't have felt like a good move. Of those who remained in Baghdad, 350 men, women and children were now sleeping in the embassy, spread out between the ballroom and the lawn, around which a barricade of cars was formed in a semicircle, intertwined with barbed wire. The telephone line was cut, and from then on, the embassy was cut off from all telephonic communication except with the Iraqi foreign-affairs minister, although radio communications continued for a few days until the embassy's radio transmitter was confiscated. Outside, Iraqi soldiers stood guard, letting no one in or out, while police launches patrolled up and down the river at the end of the garden. Ambassador Cornwallis ordered the burning of all the secret archives and most ciphers, and food was rationed.

Freya Stark was one of the British nationals besieged. She described it as having a 'Lucknow atmosphere', as elderly diplomats were rota-ed to patrol the boundaries armed from an embassy stock of fifty rifles, some of which were clearly props as they had been found by the Entertainments committee stored in the top of a grand piano. They all prepared for the worst.

In Habbaniya, just before midday, Smart sent a response to the Iraqi commander. He said that since the terms of the 1930 Treaty were a political matter, it had been referred back to the Ambassador in Baghdad. Meanwhile, he 'recommended' that

Colonel Said withdrew his forces to avoid any 'accidental problems'. He followed up with a message copied to Cornwallis in Baghdad, Air HQ in Cairo, his boss General Auchinleck at India Command in Delhi, and the Air Ministry in London, giving the gist of the second message received from the Iraqi Commander, and his reply. He said that he had decided not to issue an ultimatum to the Iraqi Commander, in view of the policy so far pursued by HQ RAF Middle East, and that offensive action would be deferred until the Iraqis opened fire. An immediate directive was asked for, together with the status of reinforcements.

A third message came from the Iraqis at around 13:30, agreeing to do nothing hostile provided Habbaniya did likewise. Smart responded by asking the Iraqi forces to stay well clear of the perimeter when darkness fell, to avoid any incidents.

Signals continued to flash back and forth during the afternoon between the various British headquarters. Cornwallis said he was in favour of an air attack against the Iraqis as they had committed an Act of War, but that he advised waiting for a firm decision from London. Meanwhile, he continued to demand that Rashid Ali pull his forces back. Smart asked advice on what form an ultimatum to the Iraqis should take, or should he just launch a preemptive strike? Cornwallis again suggested waiting for London to respond, adding that he sympathised with Smart's predicament.

Late in the day, Air Marshal Tedder replied from Cairo to say he was sending ten Wellington bombers to Basrah. He advised that, subject to the Ambassador's view, they should be used as soon as the Iraqis opened fire - though Smart realised that with a minimum of three hours flying time from Basrah, this risked being too late. Meanwhile Iraqi troops continued to stream down the road from Fallujah and on to the Plateau.

It was not until the early hours of May 1st that more substantive messages of advice started to arrive, though they were not the firm instruction that Smart craved. Instead he got a message from Auchinleck to advise that, in his judgement, Smart should attack at once; a new message from Cornwallis, to say he would back whatever Smart decided to do; and a signal, finally, from the Foreign Office in London, copied to Cornwallis and Smart, saying that the situation should be cleared up, and to do so, they were free to make any decision they saw fit, including air action.

For a few hours, Smart dithered. His instinct told him to issue an ultimatum, but he realised he needed a full day's daylight to act if the ultimatum was not respected, and moreover the ultimatum had to give the Iraqis the minimum amount of time to prepare for its expiry. Doubtless the Iraqi commander would need to refer the ultimatum back to Baghdad, so the Iraqis could quite rightly point out they needed time to get a decision. The only way it would work was if the ultimatum was issued very early in the morning - say at 05:00 - with a maximum expiry of three hours, giving him the whole day from 08:00 to go into action. Besides, he also had to evacuate the women and children who had arrived from Baghdad. The first group of them were flown out to Basrah for their onward journey to India on the two BOAC flying boats from Lake Habbaniya that morning. Smart messaged his superiors and the ambassador this plan around midday.

Cornwallis replied that he should start air action at once, but Smart rejected this as he had only half a day remaining. Then at 17:30 Tedder, in Cairo, replied, giving Smart two alternatives:

> • *To announce the continuance of full flying training, and to put the announcement into effect. If this caused the Iraqis to open fire, air attack should be commenced against Government offices in Baghdad and at Rashid Camp.*

> • *To give a three hour ultimatum for the removal of the Iraqi forces surrounding Habbaniya. If this ultimatum was not accepted, air action should be taken firstly against Government Offices in Baghdad.*

However, by the time the signal arrived (it had taken some time to decipher), the local village of Sin el Dhibban had been occupied by Iraqi troops, and more were starting to appear on the Plateau. They now numbered nearly 9,000, two full brigades. Dunford Wood, with new instructions to keep above 2,000ft, went up on a recce flight in an Audax and by this time at least twenty-five field guns and howitzers were dug in facing the camp. Smart was rapidly running out of options, and knew that he would need every hour of daylight he could get. Emboldened by a message that ten Wellington bombers had arrived in Basrah, he called a meeting of the base commanders for 20:00 that evening. This time a new officer was present, Colonel Ouvry Roberts, who had flown in from Basrah that morning to assess the situation.

The meeting didn't last long, and was followed by a last signal to the Ambassador, repeated to Air HQ Cairo, HQ RAF India, GOC Basrah, and the Air Ministry in London, in which Smart explained that the deterioration in the situation now made it necessary to attack the following morning without an ultimatum. It was a decision that would be the second key factor in deciding the coming battle. Dunford Wood's last entry for the day was:

> *"21:30: C/O has told us we attack Iraqis tomorrow.*
> *Under Ling as C/O our flight is ordered to stand by*
> *from 05:00."* [5]

~

1. The War Diaries of Colin Dunford Wood, Vol 1, 30th April 1941.
2. In Every Place: The RAF Cars in the Middle East, Nigel Warwick, page 277.
3. Iraq 1941, Robert Lyman, p 37.
4. The Baghdad Set - Iraq through the eyes of British Intelligence, by Adrian O'Sullivan, pp 53-54.
5 .The War Diaries of Colin Dunford Wood, Vol 1, 1st May 1941.

War!

"If you have to strike, strike hard. Use all necessary force."

Message received from Churchill, 04:00, May 2nd

As THE GROUND CREW BEGAN, in the darkness, to crank the propellers of the motley collection that made up the Habbaniya Striking Force - the Audaxes on the polo ground, the Oxfords, Gordons and Gladiators on the main airfield - the Iraqis must have wondered what was going on. Many of them were preparing their prayer mats for the first prayer of that Friday, their holy day, in the half hour that remained before sunrise just after 05:00. It was also their boy King's sixth birthday, as the first Baghdad radio broadcast of the day reminded its listeners.[1] A warming light was just beginning to suffuse the desert to the east.

However, it didn't take them long to understand, as the distant sputtering of aircraft engines coming from the camp below was slowly drowned out by a very different and more menacing sound: low, insistent and gradually rising in volume, it appeared to be approaching from the south. Within minutes ten huge Wellington bombers droned overhead and the first bombs started to thwump as they exploded on the desert floor.

The Iraqis abandoned their prayer mats within minutes and scrambled to open fire with the big guns they had dug in on the edge of the escarpment. As the Oxfords and Fairey Gordons sneaked out of the camp perimeter gate to the airfield one by one, banking steeply to the right as soon as they were in the air, flashes started to appear in the semi-darkness, and the first shells whistled overhead. The Audaxes taking off from the polo ground were slightly better protected.

It had been a close run thing to get the planes bombed up in time. Late into the night, ground crew had been rounded up from their various defensive duties around the camp. When Smart had issued the attack order the previous evening, he had flatly refused to excuse them from duty, so the squadron commanders had had to disobey the order and had gone to fetch them themselves.

Now, as daylight grew stronger, the air above the Plateau began to resemble a wasp's nest. Dudgeon vividly described the scene:

> "Aircraft of five different types and speeds, clustering and jockeying over an area not much larger than a minor golf course. It was a hairy experience. In my Oxford I would peer down into the dusk, trying to distinguish a juicy target like a gun-emplacement - and an Audax would swoop past at some crazy angle. Or a Wellington would sail majestically across my bows, giving me heart failure and leaving my machine bucketing about in its slipstream." [2]

The bright yellow Oxfords flew high and steady at 1,000ft, bomb aimers carefully timing their runs, while the Audaxes swooped low as dive bombers, releasing their bombs from one wing at 200ft, coming back to offload the second wing, and then swooping up and away and back to base for rearming. It was a particularly hairy operation in an Audax - a brass lever on the right side of the cockpit released the bombs from the right wing, while a lever on the left did the same for the left wing. In order to keep control of the aircraft, the pilot had to keep one hand on the stick, so he was forced to release one wing at a time. Inevitably this upset

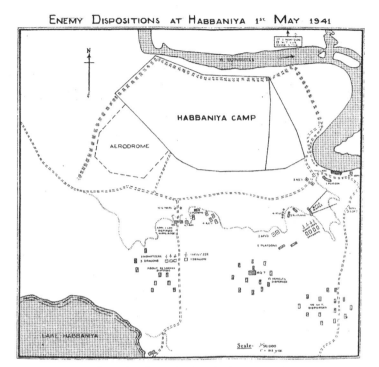

*Operational map showing the disposition of
Iraqi forces besieging Habbaniya.*

the plane's balance and as soon as one wing's bomb was released, the machine would veer over at a crazy angle until the pilot could regain control.

Meanwhile, the air gunner in the rear cockpit had challenges of his own. In order to prevent the Lewis gun accidentally shooting up the tail of the aircraft, bars were fitted on the mount to prevent the gun aiming directly backwards. However, this meant that the gunner could only fire to left or right, depending on the configuration - to swap sides, the gun had to be manually lifted over the bar and reattached to the ring. Woe betide an Audax that was attacked by an enemy aircraft from dead astern.

Coming back to land was equally nerve racking, not just due to the congestion, but because the pilots would be landing in direct line of fire of the Iraqi guns just five hundred yards away. For the planes based on the main airfield, it involved flying in low from the other side of the camp, hugging trees and buildings for protection, and then banking sharply at the last moment to approach from between the hangars.

As for the Audaxes, they had to land on the pocket handkerchief of the polo ground, coming in below tree height and then, at the final approach, lifting a few feet to clear the bushy casuarinas at the edge of the field and swinging round in a tight turn, swishing their tail fins like crazy to slow them down before they smashed into the the tents on the far side.

The turnaround was quick. The planes would be checked for bullet holes or shrapnel damage, patched up if necessary, and bombed up again, while the crews raced to the operations room - which for those on the polo ground was nearly half a mile away - to report what they had seen or hit. Gun emplacements were marked on a big map, new targets given out. Then out again, grabbing a cold beer from a zinc lined parachute bag to quench their thirst (Dunford Wood recorded that the C/O was fussing about the amount of empty bottles at one point, and asked for them to be cleared away), to find their planes once more readied for take-off, the ground crew keeping an eye out for a runway empty of others taking off or landing. As soon as it was clear, on a hand signal from the ground crew, they would taxi out again, and then race as fast as they were able towards the perimeter gate through the hail of shells and machine gun fire that the Iraqis were continuing to fling into the camp. It was a constant rotation, relentless, one in, one out, every few minutes. Occasionally an ambulance would pull up onto the airfield to carry away an injured airman, or a plane would limp to a halt, riddled with bullets.

Pilots had to learn tactics in real time. After the first few bombing runs by the ancient Fairey Gordon bombers had proved inaccurate, the flight commander, Flight Lieutenant David Evans, devised a new plan. His 250 lb bombs were fitted with safety devices to ensure that they fell at least 200ft before exploding, to avoid fatal blowback that could have destroyed the plane. This meant they had to be dropped from height, with a high chance of missing the target. Evans decided to experiment by removing the safety devices and relying solely on a seven second delay fuse, allowing him to dive down to within twenty feet of the ground before dropping his bombs with pinpoint accuracy and then having seven seconds to swoop away before they exploded. It proved effective. Dunford Wood recounted his experience that first day in his diary. He managed four sorties, two as a gunner, two as a pilot:

"I went up at sunrise in the back of Broadhurst's Audax, without a parachute like a fool, and we drop 20 lb bombs on the guns in conjunction with Oxfords and Wellingtons from Shaibah. I use the rear gun on an escaping lorry, but it's so damn hard when pulling out of a dive.

Next sortie I go up with Broughton, but we go too low and I feel something tug at my sleeve. Then liquid comes back over me, which to my horror I find to be blood. I can't see out of my goggles so stand up and find Jimmy B. in front is shot through the face and blood pouring out like a perforated petrol tank. I buckle on my parachute, but luckily he is fully conscious and we land on the polo pitch OK. I am a bit shaken and we then get shelled on the polo ground and in the mess, without much effect. Ling, Garner and Broughton get shot, and Chico Walsh with two pupils Skelton and Robinson is shot down in flames in an Oxford.

Tents erected on the Polo ground for the pilots and ground crews.

*Dan Cremin orders us four to do a continual patrol to
Baghdad with R/T. I do one at about 11am, and over
Fallujah Plain meet three Gladiators, but they pass me
by and I take it they are ours. I see 13 troop lorries and
do a little front gunning, though not very successfully."* [3]

Front gunning was a skilled job in an Audax, and Dunford
Wood had not yet received much training. The .303 Vickers
machine gun was powerful alright, but knowing how to go low
enough for accuracy while giving yourself enough time to pull
up before hitting the ground was a fine art. The RAF used to joke
about it. There was a polished human skull on the mantlepiece of
the Officer's Mess in Basra with a little brass plaque on which was
engraved *'Winner of the 1937 Front-Gunnery Contest'.*[4] The pace
was relentless:

> *"For man or machine the rule was the same:
> minor damage, or minor wounds that were not
> incapacitating, keep cracking. No respite - no breaks.*

106

*Anyone who had no more than a flesh wound returned
to the attack as fast as the planes could be re-armed and
re-crewed. The terms 'minor damage' or 'flesh wounds'
might have been stretched a bit and not assessed in a
normal RAF manner - but our situation was far from
normal. Ground-fire was both intense and accurate.
Every machine was damaged to some extent but the
record went to an Audax flown by Flight Lieutenant
Dan Cremin. He brought his aircraft back from a
single ten minute sortie with 52 new bullet holes in it.
Miraculously, he had no personal bullet holes through
him, but his pupil gunner was less fortunate. He was
carted off to hospital..."* [5]

Then, early afternoon, the Iraqi air force appeared, flying from
Hinaidi air base in Baghdad:

*"We get shot up and bombed in the camp by Bredas,
Savoia Marchettis, Northrops and "Peggy" Audaxes,
but no damage round me. These Iraqis have guts I
must say. We are a bit windy about these Bredas, and
we think of ours as a "suicide patrol" – we are sitting
meat for them, we haven't been taught the slightest
thing about air combat.*

*Pete (Gillespy) goes off at 3 and at 4 we get worried
as he hasn't been heard of for an hour. At 4.30 Ian
(Pringle) goes off on the patrol and finds his burnt
out plane in the desert near Fallujah. He is himself
attacked by a Breda with tracer but escapes.*

*I do a patrol to Najaf in the evening, windy as hell. I
see a Gladiator and am off "through the gate" without
waiting to see whose it was."* [6]

Casualties that day were heavy. Gillespy was the first of the Musketeers to go. He was shot down in flames in an Oxford, killed alongside his crew, both pupils. In addition to Gillespy, nine other 4 SFTS pilots - about a quarter of those available - had been killed or wounded by the end of the day. Of the four Wing Commanders, Ling did not last beyond the morning, rushed to hospital with bullet wounds, and Silyn-Roberts was also incapacitated. Holder was shot down twice during the day, but survived. Only Hawtrey was left to command the Audaxes. In addition, over two hundred shells had landed on the camp, and at least seven aircraft were destroyed on the ground. One of these was a Wellington bomber.

Of the ten Wellingtons, nine had returned to Shaibah so beat up as to be unserviceable the next day, but the tenth had had to make an emergency landing at Habbaniya after being hit in one engine during a low level attack on the Plateau. It came to halt in full view of the Iraqi guns, and although an attempt was made to tow it into cover, with the help of a section of Armoured cars, it was soon bracketed by Iraqi shellfire and destroyed.

Elsewhere, the Iraqis tried to breach the camp perimeter but were beaten off by the No 1 Armoured Car company and a company of Assyrian Levies with Boys anti-tank rifles, but it was a narrow escape. As Aircraftman Charles Spybey, a wireless operator in one of the armoured cars, described it:

> "A dozen Iraqi armoured cars ventured across the open ground in the afternoon, but six of our cars went out and gave battle. We completely riddled eight of them with armour piercing bullets, and the other four fled... It would have been the easiest thing in the world for the Iraqis to cross the open strip of ground, about half a mile in length, between the Plateau and the camp, during the first night and wipe us out completely..." [7]

However, the camp was not just vulnerable to a night ground attack. Iraqi shellfire could easily have incapacitated the camp's water supplies. Although the continuous bombing runs of the Audaxes, Oxfords and Gordons that first day succeeded in reducing the bombardment, there was still a huge risk, and everyone expected the Iraqis to target the water tower.

For example around midday, an Iraqi battery set up two 3.7 inch howitzers across the Euphrates to the north of the camp, behind the one of the Bunds, and started shelling from an even shorter range. No 8 (Kurdish) company of Levies was sent across by boat to try and silence them, but were beaten back by machine gun fire, and it was left to a flight of Audaxes later in the day to finally put them out of action. Spybey recalled the barrage and the fear they all had:

> *"Hundreds of shells were pumped into the camp... later in the day, the Iraqi air force sent their own aircraft over and bombed us, one bomb hitting my billet. Nobody was in at the time. Our water supply was stored in a huge tower, and we realised that if it was hit we might have a hard time. I was ordered to go to all the huts in our section and fill all the baths and sinks and buckets with water and in doing so had to duck the gunfire which rained down on us continually - really scary!"*

Flight Lieutenant Ted Frith, the Company Adjutant, was even more concerned:

> *"We had the idea they would go for the water tower. They only had to pierce it and we would have been out of business, but they didn't, because they wanted the camp."* [8]

Was that the reason? It seems that cowed by the ferocity of the RAF's pre-emptive strike, and still perhaps in thrall to the British, the Iraqis lacked the ruthlessness that they needed to overwhelm Habbaniya. It also transpired that the Iraqi troops had been told by their officers that their advance to the Plateau was just a training exercise, so they were totally unprepared for the surprise onslaught that was unleashed against them. As for their superiors, they had fully expected the British to surrender or negotiate.

That evening, Smart called another meeting of his senior commanders. After the day's action, the RAF contingent was somewhat depleted, the Air Striking Force being represented by Savile, Dudgeon and Hawtrey. Despite the valiant efforts of the pilots and crews during the day, the Iraqis were still firmly ensconced on the Plateau. Reinforcements were still arriving. When they reviewed the toll on their own assets the results were sobering. Of about a hundred personnel that were involved in the air as pilots and aircrew, thirteen had been killed and twenty wounded - an attrition rate of a third. The thirty-nine pilots who had started the day were down to twenty-nine. Around a third of the flying school's sixty-four serviceable aircraft were either destroyed or put out of action. In total they had flown 193 sorties, an average of five sorties per pilot, of which sixty sorties were flown by Ling's 'C' Squadron of Audaxes, who dropped 450 bombs.[9] Of their eleven Audaxes, five had been rendered unserviceable by anti-aircraft fire. How long could they keep this up? Days at the most.

The meeting was dispiriting: Smart was out of ideas, and started blaming the 'powers that be' for not sending him reinforcements in time. It was to be more of the same in the morning. The only new decision of note was to finish evacuating the women and children at first light in the morning, under cover of the 05:00 attack. Arrangements were made with 31 Squadron in Shaibah to send their DC3 transport aircraft to pick them up.

Meanwhile Smart sent a fresh flurry of signals to London, Cairo and the embassy in Baghdad asking for an ETA on reinforcements. Worryingly, the Embassy in Baghdad had gone silent, and the phone lines were dead.

That night, the ground crew patched up the remaining planes as best they could, to ready them for action again at 05:00, while the pilots tried to get some sleep. The Levies were ordered to maintain patrols in no-man's-land, to deter any night attack. Meanwhile the Iraqis started up a new barrage at midnight, which continued until 03:00, so any sleep, for anyone, proved hard to come by.

~

1. Before fleeing a few days earlier, the Regent had sent the young King Faisal 11 to Mosul in the north of the country in the care of his English nanny. When he resurfaced a month later to welcome the British back into Baghdad, he was photographed in a spotless white shirt and shorts, crisply ironed.
2. The War That Never Was, Tony Dudgeon, pp 81-83.
3. The War Diaries of Colin Dunford Wood, Vol 1, 2nd May 1941.
4. The War That Never Was, Tony Dudgeon, p121.
5. The War That Never Was, Tony Dudgeon, pp 84-85.
6. The War Diaries of Colin Dunford Wood, Vol 1, 3rd May 1941.
7. In Every Place -RAF Armoured Cars in the Middle East, Nigel Warwick, p 280.
8. In Every Place -RAF Armoured Cars in the Middle East, Nigel Warwick, p282.
9. 'C' squadron Historical Record, P/O Haig and P/O Dunford Wood..

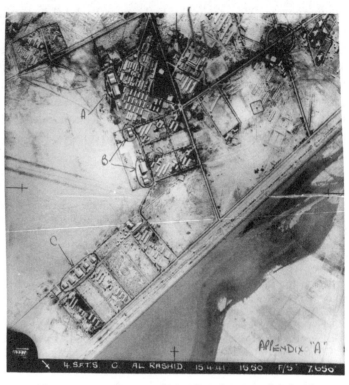

*Photo-reconnaissance map of Hinaidi air base in Baghdad with
potential targets marked out for the pilots of 4 SFTS.*

Reactions

In Baghdad, the eruption of hostilities on May 2nd had caught Rashid Ali and the Red Fox by surprise. From early on the morning of the attack, the radio blared out martial music, while Rashid Ali made an address to the nation, urging calm. The Ministry of Propaganda jammed the BBC, and broadcast messages making reference to Britain's infringement of Iraqi sovereignty and having broken the terms of the treaty, along with calls for the 'liberation of our homeland' from 'British imperialism':

> *"Mothers, brothers, wives, know that you are serving this nation. We are conscious of a just and noble cause."* [1]

German propaganda broadcasts dominated the airwaves, while prominent Baghdadis were wheeled out to denounce the British imperialists in the press. Radio Bari from Italy broadcast congratulations on the King's birthday, but expressed concern that the King's health was entrusted to a Scottish doctor, Dr 'Sinbad' Sindersen, who had cared for the two previous Kings, both of whom had died in suspicious circumstances.

There was a total blackout. Schools were closed, and banks ordered not to allow people to withdraw money. Members of the Futuwwah,[2] the youth movement modelled on the Hitler youth, took up patrolling the streets, and people were arrested for anything that looked suspicious: for example a Jewish student carrying an English book was accused of spying, and a French violin teacher of carrying a radio. A woman whose gold button flashed in the sunlight was accused of signalling to the British Embassy.

Baghdad was jittery. The embassy continued in lockdown. Their radio had been confiscated, and although they had a spare one to receive news from the BBC, they had no way of communicating with Habbaniya or knowing what was going on. Their electricity was cut off and it was swelteringly hot in the day without fans ('no light, fans, bells or ironing' was how Freya Stark described the inconvenience), and food had to be brought in under police guard, on payment of a baksheesh[3]. Not long after the siege started, a mob approached, banging drums and chanting anti-British slogans. An Iraqi communique claimed twenty-nine British planes had been destroyed on the ground. There was no reason to disbelieve it. Stark wrote:

> *"The Chancery is a bonfire, mountains of archive being burnt in the court, prodded by the staff with rakes. State of siege has been going on for three days. Dormitory upstairs; uprooted women. Petrol tins of sand everywhere for bombs; cars parked on lawn; men sprawling asleep round the blue tiled fountain in the hall to be cool; We have a big V on the lawn in white sheets to tell the air (the RAF) that we are lost to news."[4]*

They were particularly worried about the women and children who had been evacuated to Habbaniya, from whom they had heard nothing.

§

A thousand miles to the west in Cairo, 2nd May marked the beginning of the end of Wavell's Middle East Command. When he had originally been asked for reinforcements for Iraq after Rashid Ali's coup in early April, he could have been forgiven for cavilling

- at that point, his situation looked dire, with Greece under attack and Tobruk threatened by Rommel. In any case, Iraq had only recently been transferred to India command and was now their responsibility.

However, by late April Whitehall's point-of-view had radically shifted. Unaware of Hitler's plans towards Russia, it looked very much as if all German roads were suddenly leading to the Middle East. With Libya occupied by Rommel, Greece being overrun, and a Nazi inspired coup d'etat in Baghdad, it seemed that a German move into Syria and Iraq would be the next logical step. Moreover, Churchill well understood that a poor British response in Iraq might alienate the Turks, and, in turn, send them into the German camp. As Auchinleck stated, *"the fall of Iraq to the Axis would mean the loss of oil fields, and the possibility of Turkey swinging towards them."*

The attack on Habbaniya, coming just days after the fall of Greece, ratcheted up the pressure. Again London cabled Wavell for help:

> *"In view of situation in Iraq, which is not what we visualised when India took responsibility, it seems operational command should now pass temporarily to Mid East, whence alone immediate assistance can be given. This will take place forthwith, unless you see strong objections..."*

As John Connell noted in his biography of Wavell:

> *"Thus the control of a crucial operation was precipitously transferred from the commander who had both the will and the forces to exercise it effectively, to one who was most evidently reluctant to assume it, whose forces on several fronts were strained to the limit.."* [5]

Wavell later wrote in his memoirs:

"I always disliked Iraq - the country, the people and the military commitment... it blew up at the worst possible time for me, when I had the Western Desert, Crete, East Africa and Syria on my hands, and no troops." [6]

The day the message arrived, Wavell was out in the desert dealing with Rommel's latest attempt to take Tobruk. On his return he confided his thoughts to the High Commissioner for Egypt, Miles Lampson, as Lampson recorded in his diaries:

"Wavell told me this morning that he saw no alternative but to treat with the Iraqis. I was horrified..." [7]

Consequently Wavell's first response to the Chiefs of Staff on 3rd May was stinging:

"I have consistently warned you that no assistance could be given to Iraq from Palestine... commitment in Iraq should be avoided. My forces are stretched to the limit everywhere... I do not see how I can possibly accept military responsibility." [8]

Then, three hours later, realising he needed to strike a more constructive tone, he cabled again to say he would see what force could be improvised from Palestine, but that in his opinion it would be too weak and too late to relieve Habbaniya, as it would take some days to organise and then needed to cross five hundred miles of desert. Instead, he suggested the only way to solve the Iraq crisis was through diplomatic means, perhaps mediated by Turkey or America.

A response to this latest message took some time to put together in London, since it was the weekend, but it was clear that

Churchill was angry. Wavell signalled again, to say he had had no response. Finally, in the evening, the Chiefs of Staff replied. They firmly rejected his suggestion of mediation:

> *"Your actions will therefore now be directed to implement the following policy:*
>
> *• The active defence of Habbaniya must be maintained by all possible means.*
> *• Preparation for sending a force to restore situation... must be pressed on.*
>
> *Our Ambassador in Iraq is being instructed to continue to exercise all possible pressure on Iraqi Government. For this purpose he can threaten the following action should situation develop into active war:*
>
> *• Air bombardment of Baghdad.*
> *• Destruction of Akrutiyah dam (we are advised this is possible by air action.)*
> *• Destruction of oil pumping stations.*
> *• Complete blockade of Basrah."*

The sentence 'should situation develop into active war' was odd in this context, as active war was very much what was then going on in Iraq.

The following day was Wavell's birthday. But he was not in a birthday mood. First thing in the morning he composed his reply, and told them that their instruction "takes little account of realities. You must face facts." He explained his relief force could not be ready until the 10th, and that he was:

> *"Very doubtful whether force strong enough to relieve Habbaniya, or whether Habbaniya can prolong*

117

resistance till its arrival. I am afraid I can only regard it as an outside chance.

I feel it my duty to warn you in gravest possible terms that I consider prolongation of fighting in Iraq will seriously endanger defence of Palestine and Egypt. Apart from the weakening of strength by detachments such as above, political repercussions will be incalculable and may result in what I have spent nearly two years trying to avoid, serious internal trouble at our bases. I therefore urge again most strongly that settlement should be negotiated as soon as possible..."

This, then, was his real fear - that confronting the Iraqis would lead to a Middle East wide revolt by the Arabs against the British. It was a concern that exposed the contradiction at the heart of his role as C-in-C Middle East: to what extent was he required to be a statesman? Where did the soldier end and the politician begin? The CIGS, General Dill, was to put it succinctly to Wavell's successor:

"The fact is, the Commander in the field will always be subject to great and often undue pressure from his government. Wellington suffered from it, Haig suffered from it, Wavell suffered from it. Nothing will stop it. In fact pressure from those who alone see the picture as a whole, and carry the main responsibility, may be necessary." [9]

And this was the problem - Wavell did not see the big picture. His views were based on only a partial grasp of the reality of Iraqi and Middle Eastern politics. His tone verged on insubordination.[10]

The next day, following a meeting of the War Cabinet, the Chiefs of Staff confirmed their decision, despite his objections, to transfer responsibility for Iraq back to his Middle East Command,

and their instructions to him to organise a relief column. His slightly jovial acknowledgement of this reverse in a private message to his old friend, Sir John Dill, the CIGS, belied his exasperation:

> *"Nice baby you have landed me on my 58th birthday. Have always hated babies and Iraqis, but will do my best for the little blighter."*

It was the first time in the war that a general in theatre had been overruled by the Chiefs of Staff. To his objection that the Household Cavalry unit in Palestine, which they suggested he send, had no horses and no transport, Churchill acidly remarked:

> *"Fancy having kept the Cavalry Division in Palestine all this time without having the rudiments of a mobile column organised!"* [11]

It may have been unfair, but it was revealing. The countdown to his dismissal had begun. The Director of Military Operations at the War Office, noted in his memoirs:

> *"On the morning of 6th May, when I went to see Dill, he said 'There is a serious matter to be settled today. The Prime Minister wants to sack Wavell and put Auchinleck back into the Middle-East.'"* [12]

All this bickering between Wavell and London contrasted with the speed of response from General Auchinleck, C-in-C India, 1,500 miles away, whose force was now embedded in Basrah but of no immediate help to Habbaniya, given the flooding to the north of them. In the period it took, four days, for Wavell to start organising reinforcements, Habbaniya could well have been overrun and the Iraqis in the ascendant. Even aircraft could have made a big difference. The fact that Habbaniya survived, as we shall see, was through no help from Wavell. Indeed, its survival ironically saved him from far worse.

§

Just as the British were dithering and arguing amongst themselves, so the Germans were having similar issues. Most of the senior command were focussed on preparations for Operation Barbarossa, due to start on June 22nd after a four week delay caused by the Balkan campaign. But Rashid Ali's premature advance on Habbaniya concentrated minds, as it had in London. It might have been an unwelcome opportunity, but it was one that Ribbentrop was determined to seize. On the 3rd May he pushed Hitler again:

> *"If the available reports are correct regarding the relatively small forces the English have landed in so far, there would seem to be a great opportunity for establishing a base for warfare against England through an armed Iraq.*
>
> *A constantly expanding insurrection of the Arab world would be of the greatest help in the preparation of our decisive advance toward Egypt."*

The German embassy in Ankara reported on 5th May that:

> *"The Iraqi government requests immediate military aid. In particular a considerable number of airplanes in order to prevent further English landings and to drive the English from the airfields. The Iraqi minister asked for an answer tomorrow if in any way possible."*

The next day, Wehrmacht High Command held a conference to discuss what forces and measures they could offer. Given the urgency and the distance, the Luftwaffe was the only realistic option. There is no record of any discussion of sending the Luftwaffe's airborne division, XI. Fliegerkorps, which had just been earmarked for Crete, but they agreed to send an echelon of He-111 bombers from Rhodes, which had been positioned for action against the Suez Canal, along with some Me-110 fighter aircraft from the Balkans, and 750 tons of equipment from Syria.

Dr Rahn, the German ambassador in Paris, was given the task of organising these supplies, and he flew out to Beirut immediately after agreeing arrangements with the Vichy Government in Paris. Von Hentig had originally been proposed, but the French flatly refused to have him, considering the agitation he had caused on his last visit.

At the same time, official diplomatic relations between Germany and Iraq were restored, and Fritz Grobba was informed he was to return to Baghdad to resume his former post as ambassador. According to notes taken after this conference,[13] quick results were expected from the intervention. However, there were two conditions attached.

First, a Middle East-wide Arab revolt was to be avoided, in order to accommodate the French, who did not want unrest in Syria. Second, the Italians were to be given the bare minimum of information, both because of their sensitivity to German encroachment into their sphere of influence (as set out in the Ribbentrop-Ciano Pact of 1940), and their inability to maintain secrecy.

As with Wavell, the challenge was the delay before reinforcements could arrive. It was now a race against time, to get there before the British. An agreement was swiftly brokered with the Vichy Government, though given the urgency, the Germans were forced to give away rather more than they would have wanted. On 8 May the Paris Protocols were agreed, and they confirmed the following concessions:

(a) The stocks of French arms impounded under the terms of France's surrender, and now under Italian control in Syria, to be made available for transporting to Iraq, with 25% to be returned to the French.

(b) French assistance in the forwarding of arms shipments of other origin that arrive in Syria for Iraq;

(c) Permission for German planes, destined for Iraq, to make intermediate landings and to take on fuel in Syria;

(d) Cession to Iraq of reconnaissance, pursuit and bombing planes, as well as bombs, from the air force permitted for Syria under the armistice treaty;

(e) An airfield in Syria to be made available especially for the intermediate landing of German planes;

(f) Until such an airfield has been made available, an order to be issued to all airfields in Syria to assist German planes making intermediate landings.

In return, the Germans agreed to permit the rearmament of six French destroyers and seven torpedo boats, to relax the stringent travel and traffic regulations between the zones of France, and to arrange for a substantial reduction of the costs of occupation.

On the same day the Paris Protocols were agreed, German planes were flown to Silistra, in Rumania, to be made desert ready. In particular, their Luftwaffe swastikas were to be overpainted with Iraqi Air Force markings. Unlike the RAF, the Luftwaffe had no experience of tropical or desert conditions, and it took time to convert them - although, as we shall see, it was barely enough. From there, they flew on to Greece, where the aircrew were issued tropical uniforms and equipment, and the bombers were crammed with ammunition, rations, tents, and spare parts. However, the pilots were poorly briefed, and none of them knew what to expect when they arrived in Iraq, from where news was patchy.

~

1. Iraq Between the Two World Wars, Reeva Spector Simon pp 142-143.
2. Disparagingly referred to by the British as 'the footwear', on account of their black marching boots.
3. A bribe.
4. Dust in the Lions Paw, Freya Stark, pp 89-90.
5. Wavell, John Connell, p 434.
6. Of Generals and Gardens, Peter Coats, p 106.
7. Of Generals and Gardens, Peter Coats, p 106.
8. The Crucible of War, Barrie Pitt, p281.
9. The Chief, Ronald Lewin, p44.
10. The third of his famous pre-war Lees-Knowles lectures was titled 'The Soldier and the Statesman', and dealt with the necessity for senior commanders to understand and work in sync with their political masters. It was clear by his response to the crisis in Iraq that he had not learned the lessons of his own lecture.
11. The Crucible of War, Barrie Pitt, p283.
12. The Business of War, Major General Sir John Kennedy.
13. German Exploitation of Arab Nationalist Movements in World War II by Hellmuth Felmy and Walter Warlimont.

Habbaniya's aircraft hangars under attack.

Hanging on

IN IRAQ, RAF HABBANIYA WAS HOLDING out - just. After the evening briefing held by Smart on the 2nd May, the last Dudgeon remembers being held, he and Savile decided to rearrange the remaining aircraft into two wings, and the Gladiators were moved to the polo ground, to bolster the Audaxes that were left, now under the command of Hawtrey. In addition to their role as roving fighter defence, the Gladiators were to take over reconnaissance responsibilities, and the remaining three Musketeers were to become fully operational pilots, now under Flight Lieutenant Dan Cremin in place of the injured Ling.

At 05:00 on the 3rd, air attacks were launched once more on the Iraqi troops on the Plateau by the Audaxes and Oxfords, as cover for the arrival at first light of three DC2 aircraft of 31 Squadron flying in from Shaibah with supplies. They had aboard an artificer, with tools to recommission the two ancient howitzers that stood ceremonially outside Air HQ, and a crate of 3.3 inch shells.[1]

Having landed and offloaded, the turnaround had to be swift. The remaining evacuees from Baghdad scrambled aboard, along with the camp's most seriously wounded. As the planes prepared to leave, armoured cars of the No 1 Armoured car company raced up and down alongside the runway to stir up clouds of dust, so that the planes could taxi and take off obscured from the Iraqi gunners on the Plateau. Miraculously, they all got off unharmed.

Meanwhile, the battle raged on, directed in the air by Savile, and on the ground by Colonel Roberts. Over 72 hours, a relentless schedule of sorties were flown, against a widening choice of targets and with a diminishing band of pilots. More Wellington bombers arrived at Shaibah to replace the ones that were still out of action, and it was decided to take the fight to the Iraqi air force. Three Wellington bombers took off from Shaibah at dawn and joined up with Habbaniya's Audaxes and Oxfords to attack Hinaidi air base in Baghdad, dropping 7,000 lb of bombs. The following day, eight more Wellingtons arrived from Shaibah for a second run, dropping a further 15,000 lb. This time, quite unexpectedly, they were joined by four Blenheims from 203 Squadron under the command of Squadron Leader Pike, that had flown in from Cairo, supported by two Hurricane escorts.[2] They provided a powerful reinforcement. The Embassy in Baghdad had a grandstand view of both these operations against the Iraqi air base. Freya Stark recalls seeing 'a very beautiful sight' from the embassy garden where she had been sleeping, at 04:00:

> "In the faintest beginning of light...a great Wellington, slowly sailing along at 1,000 feet up the river, very dark against the green sky and the sleeping houses."[3]

Photographic evidence afterwards showed that twenty-nine Iraqi aircraft were damaged or destroyed on the ground - a third of their airforce.

Later in the day on the 4th, another attack was made by Audaxes and Gladiators on the Iraqi air force at Hinaidi, where a further twenty-one Iraqi aircraft were surprised on the ground. Fourteen of them were damaged or destroyed for the loss of one Audax. Meanwhile other elements of the Air Striking Force targeted the Baghdad-Fallujah road along which supplies were arriving for the Iraqi troops.

Iraqi shells, however, continued to rain down. Dunford Wood wrote on the 4th:

> *"Shelling last night from 9.30-12.30 and then again at 4am. I lie quaking in my bed, but they don't seem to do much damage. All the bearers (servants) are hiding under their beds in the civil cantonment and nothing is done. A plane is up continuously tonight, so hope there will be no more shelling and I will get some sleep."* [4]

This was part of a new tactic to try and deter night time shelling. At dusk, an aircraft would drop time delay bombs set to go off at random intervals during the night, followed by a standing patrol of roving Audaxes in the moonlight. Then, around midnight, when the moon set and it became pitch black, an Oxford would go up to circle the Plateau, to be relieved after two hours by another one. It was easy to spot the gun flashes on the ground, to give them a target to aim for. Otherwise, in the absence of Iraqi artillery fire, a 20 lb bomb dropped once every 15 minutes served to keep Iraqi heads down.

Night flying after the moon had set was a hairy business, as Dunford Wood had already found out in training, and doubly hairy with no runway lights due to the blackout. Oxfords had been chosen for this task over the Audaxes because they were the only planes with landing lights, which could be switched on with minimal risk for a few seconds when the altimeter read fifty feet, to check proximity to the ground and make sure they were coming down on the runway, before being switched off again on touch down. The most unnerving part was take off - without airfield lights, the pilots had to point their aircraft into the darkness using a compass bearing, careful to avoid the burnt out carcass of the Wellington bomber that had been destroyed on the first day of the battle, and an Oxford wreck beyond it, and then time their run for exactly four and a half minutes - by which time they estimated they would be approaching the end of the runway - before opening the throttles for a blind take off. There were only three experienced pilots fit for this task - those who had been sent to Habbaniya after operations 'for a rest'. Dudgeon was one of them. He described having got away with it with a vast amount of luck. Of the other two pilots, one lost his nerve and refused to do it anymore, and the other, having not taxi-ed out far enough onto the runway and turning for his take off too early, clipped the top of the embankment at the end of his run, somersaulted into the desert and caught fire. Both he and his pupil-observer were killed. As Dudgeon wrote later, it was a bit like that children's song, ten green bottles, where after each verse, one accidentally fell...

For the rest of the Air Striking Force, the whole routine would start again at dawn. The pace was punishing. The pilots flew from 05:00 until 20:00 when it got dark, with a few rota-ed for the moonlight patrols, and then the work started on patching up the planes again by the fitters and riggers, while the squadron commanders worked out a rota for the following day, based on how many serviceable aircraft - and pilots - there were left. Most of the pilots and crew did not get away, after reporting in, until about 22:00, when they scrounged whatever they could find to eat in the mess before bed at midnight and up again at 04:00 to get ready for the next day's action. Dunford Wood describes the relentless nature of the fight:

"More shelling at dawn and at 9am today, despite patrols in the air all night. Pat Weir and a platoon of King's Own do a successful raid Dhibban way last night without any casualties. I am on at dawn, 4.15, then off 5-9, on 9-1, off 1-5 and on again to dusk. Mostly sitting around in our operations tent while "Doug" Baker presides with three telephones, fixes everything up, serves beer and washes up the glasses, besides having the tent cleaned out. With the help of W.O. Shawn Sheagh, R.E., we snaffle some ice to keep the beer cold in a zinc lined parachute box which is the frigidaire.

I go up before lunch to bomb four cars in a copse and undershoot them. Then at dusk Dan, Gordon Arthur, Alan and myself go up to spot the guns at their dusk shelling. I am just coming home as the sun has disappeared when I see other planes in the air, so reckon I had better stay up a bit longer. I turn and notice a flash in a copse. I climb up and drop four bombs on the wrong copse, then four bombs on the right one (near "Camel Turn"), all of which overshoot. But I get in three good long bursts with my front gun at it, and Cpl Sanderson in the back does some good work with his Lewis gun. I report to P/O Shotter in the ops rooms, find the copse on a photographic map, and they are all pleased as it is a new one. I then find there was no shelling at the time I saw the flash, so it can't have been a gun!" [5]

However, the combination of constant day bombing and standing night patrols was beginning to have an effect. As the official report made clear after the event, this strategy "produced a curious reversal of the tactical situation. For whereas Habbaniya was itself cut off from outside help or supply, except by air, its garrison was now in effect besieging the Iraqi forces on the Plateau dominating the Cantonment."[6]

At 10:00 on the 4th, the Intelligence branch of headquarters staff issued the first daily camp bulletin, *'so that everyone can be kept up to date with events.'* Seventy-seven copies were produced, including ten each for the Aircraft Depot, 4 SFTS, the Armoured Cars, the Levies, the King's Own and the hospital. The first issue covered events from 2nd and 3rd and noted that over 86,000 lb bombs had been dropped, and that four gun positions and three A.A. positions had been silenced, along with a tank, transport and a horse drawn artillery unit.

"There can be no doubt," it went on, *"that heavy bombing carried out by our aircraft ... inflicted heavy casualties on the enemy,"* - evidenced by the appeal issued by the Baghdad radio that all doctors should register with the Committee of Health within three days - *"demoralised his gun crews, and prevented more than a desultory and largely ineffective shelling of Habbaniya; their effect, as a glance at the shell holes will confirm, has been negligible."*

The report ended with a very British note of encouragement:

"It is worth remembering that three-fourths of the chances of success depend on morale and a confident spirit, and only one fourth on material conditions."

On the face of it, those material conditions were very much still in the Iraqis favour. But in Baghdad, the first radio broadcast from Rashid Ali was defensive in tone:

> *"To the people of Iraq. We were forced to take defensive measures, and the military operations which have begun are continuing with successes to our Army. The noble Iraqi nation is requested to remain quiet, proving its political maturity, and confidence in our national forces."*[7]

The British had been in Iraq since 1920, and their presence was embedded in the fabric of Iraqi life. Most Iraqis held their own political masters in low esteem, and many had for years relied on the British to help exercise restraint on them. So Rashid Ali was right to be nervous. There was no sense of nationwide support for the actions he had taken, so extensive efforts were taken to whip up enthusiasm. On the 4th Rashid Ali addressed the nation again:

> *"Our forces draw the ring around the aerodrome of Habbaniya steadily closer. The garrison is continually being bombarded by our artillery. It is presumed that the enemy will be beaten. Many fires were caused in ammunition and fuel dumps. At the Western border of our oil fields our recce troops went into action and are in contact with the high command. Our troops have contacted the enemy and operations are carried out according to plan."*

This was followed by a Baghdad news bulletin, organised by the Red Fox, which had a very different tone:

> *"O believers in God and in his Prophet. Fighting is written for you, to free yourselves and your country, collaborating together as one man supporting your noble Government under the leadership of Rashid Ali and with the support of your brave and courageous army...I call you, all Iraqi people, to the battlefield, to the scene of honour, shoulder to shoulder against the tyrant, the British who started the aggression against us."*

In response, the Regent made a broadcast from exile in Transjordan. This did not go unnoticed in Habbaniya, and in issue

131

two of the daily bulletin on 5th May, a section entitled 'Political Background' reassured the camp:

> "There exists in Iraq a large body of public opinion friendly to Great Britain, but, at the moment, leaderless and therefore voiceless. The broadcast from Amman by the Emir Abdul'llah should do much to overcome both of these deficiencies. The young Regent is popular in the country - especially so among its youth. Fighting as we are, not against the people of Iraq but against her Government of ambitious Generals and misguided politicians, the Regent's call to arms should be welcomed by what 'John Bull' calls the man in the street, who certainly does not want to fight anyone, much less his old friend Great Britain..."

The bulletin went on to describe:

> "Successful attacks...on local military objectives by our aircraft" and attacks on Hinaidi air base that accounted for "something like 50% of the total serviceable Iraqi aircraft". Furthermore, "various pamphlets in Arabic have been dropped over Baghdad, Fallujah and military concentrations at Habbaniya."

However, what is surprising about these early bulletins is that there is no message whatsoever from the Camp Commander, Air Vice-Marshal Smart. You might expect a stirring, morale boosting note of encouragement. Instead, the text was signed off each day by a Flight Lieutenant MacDonald 'for Wing Commander, Air Staff Intelligence.' Dudgeon also reported that the 2nd May evening briefing was the last time one was held, or he saw or heard from Smart.

Rumours soon started to spread about what had happened. Dunford Wood wrote in his diary a few days later *"Old Smart had a slight car crash and packed it in with shock."* Dudgeon concurs, and that while the official story was that he had had a car accident while driving in the dark around the camp in blackout, the version that was believed in the camp was that he had had a nervous breakdown.

Although nothing was recorded about the event in the official history, the most compelling evidence came from Lady Holman, the wife of the Counsellor and deputy to the British Ambassador, who had evacuated from Baghdad. She was given accommodation in the AOC's home, Air House, when she arrived, and told Dudgeon in later years:

> *"Smart lacked the respect of his subordinates, mainly because he discussed with everybody, quite openly and freely, everything that was happening, together with his personal thoughts and plans. Then, when the attack started, he became quite hysterical. He went absolutely berserk. It was so serious that the senior doctor from the hospital gave Reggie a knock-out injection so that he was totally unaware of what was going on and could be evacuated quietly. And, which is more, I actually saw him being put on the aircraft."* [8]

Whatever the truth, it is clear that he was evacuated on one of the DC2 flights, most likely on the 4th or 5th May, and that he had been under great strain. For a month, he had had to effectively cope on his own with no clear instructions, and it was left to him to take the momentous decision, on his own responsibility, to launch the flying school's pre-emptive strike. It was a brave decision, but on the evening of the first day it looked like the gamble had failed - the Iraqis were still in position and he had lost a third of his air force.

But his departure was to have consequences about how the battle was remembered in later years. Effective command now passed to Colonel Roberts.

Smart was not the only leader unable to command the respect of his subordinates. Savile had already proved to Dudgeon that he was in the same mould as his boss. On the 3rd, Dudgeon suggested that Savile should join him on a sortie, given that he had so far studiously avoided going up in an aircraft ever since the Iraqis arrived. He did not appear keen. Dudgeon pressed him, suggesting that it would be a good idea to see for himself what his instructors and pupil pilots were having to face, that it would be good for morale. After much hesitation, Savile was eventually persuaded to join the Squadron Leader in his Oxford on one of his bombing runs. It was not a happy experience for the senior officer, and as bullets whizzed past the aircraft, he demanded to be returned, white as a sheet. In later life Dudgeon was repentant: *"I should never have done it to him.... but it was the only occasion during the whole campaign that he left the ground."* [9]

On May 5th, the two ancient artillery pieces that had stood outside Air House were finally ready to be unleashed - rumour had it that twenty-two layers of paint were removed by the artificer. They were soon in action, flinging shells back at the Iraqis on the Plateau. The BBC put out a propaganda report to the effect that heavy guns had been flown in from Basrah on specially converted aircraft. Whatever their military effectiveness, it was reasoned that they would at least have a psychological impact on the besiegers.

Although the camp was largely left alone by the Iraqi Air Force on the 5th, no doubt due to the powerful standing patrol provided by the Blenheims, which the day before had shot down two Iraqi Audaxes as they attacked the camp, the strike power of the Air Striking Force had dwindled. They carried on their round the clock pounding of Iraqi positions on the Plateau, but with less than half the bomb load they had carried on May 2nd. As they reduced in numbers, so the Iraqi forces seemed to increase, with reinforcements and supplies continuing to arrive via a ferry crossing at the village of Sin el Dhibban, four miles south of Habbaniya. In an attempt to destroy the crossing, a detachment of the King's Own was sent out to capture it, but as they advanced they came up against a determined force of two hundred Iraqi troops, well dug in. It was a discouraging reverse.

That evening, Levies patrols supported by armoured cars were sent up to reconnoitre the foothills of the escarpment. There seemed to be a lot of movement, as if the Iraqis were preparing for a big attack.

Back in the camp, Savile, Hawtrey and Dudgeon tallied up what they had left. So far, the Air Striking force had flown 445 sorties. Of the twenty-seven Oxfords that Dudgeon had started with, only four remained in flying condition, and in addition to the dead and wounded, four of the original nineteen Oxford pilots had to be taken off flying because their nerves had gone. Of the Audaxes, barely ten were airworthy. It was looking very uncertain how many planes or pilots would be able to take off on the 6th.

~

1. This had been Colonel Roberts's idea. Soon after he had flown into Habbaniya on the 1st, he had noticed these two bronze artillery pieces, captured from the Turks in the Great War, standing on the lawn of Air House. Discovering that they were covered in many years worth of paint, he had signalled Basra to send up an artificer with a set of stripping tools on the next available flight, along with suitable shells.
2. When the Blenheims first arrived at Habbaniya that morning, they had clearly not been briefed on the situation, as they approached from above the Plateau as they would have done in normal times. They managed to land, but once their engines came to a halt they were found to be riddled with bullet holes, much to the horror of the pilots.
3. Dust in the Lion's Paw, Freya Stark, p91 - 4th May 1941.
4. The War Diaries of Colin Dunford Wood, Vol 1, 4th May 1941.
5. The War Diaries of Colin Dunford Wood, Vol 1, Colin Dunford Wood.
6. Official report written by a Wing Commander Casey for Air Vice-Marshal Smart.
7. Hitler's Gulf War, Barrie James, p73.

8. The War That Never Was, Tony Dudgeon, p102.
9. Luck of the Devil, Tony Dudgeon, p 183.

The remains of the Iraqi relief column, 7th May 1941, after relentless bombing by the flying school pilots.

The Siege is Broken

THE NEXT DAY AT DAWN DUNFORD WOOD was ordered into the air with a rear gunner called Fairweather, to destroy the gun he had spotted on the Plateau the evening before, and to see if he could find evidence of the expected attack. To his surprise, the gun was no longer there, and moreover, the Plateau looked empty in the half light. He reported back to the operations room, and more aircraft were sent up to see what was going on. Sure enough, the Iraqi positions had been abandoned, and troops on foot and vehicles could be seen retreating on the far side of the Plateau. Patrols of Levies were sent up towards the escarpment. No 1 section of the

Armoured Cars Company drove up as far as the BOAC resthouse on the lake, but all they found were a few abandoned vehicles. No. 3 section joined them soon after, and they made contact with small groups of retreating Iraqi troops. By 09:00 the Plateau south of Habbaniya was reported clear of enemy troops.[1] Aircraftman Spybey remembered what happened next:

> "On the fifth day (6th May)... we proceeded out of camp - the armoured cars, the infantry, and me, in my small unprotected wireless van, across the open ground towards the Plateau...by the end of the day, all the ground on the Plateau between the camp and the lake had been cleared of the enemy and they were retreating as fast as they could."[2]

However, a large contingent of Iraqi troops had only retreated as far as Sin el Dhibban village, so the King's Own were sent in for a second attack, this time in force, supported by another section of armoured cars. The fighting was fierce. The regimental history recorded the action:

> "It was preceded by the armoured cars, which were to sweep the area before the infantry attacked. 'D' Company was directed on Dhibban village while 'B' Company moved around to the right. Not a shot was fired at the armoured cars, so (the King's Own) advanced and came almost up to the village where, contrary to expectation, the enemy was found to be well dug in and camouflaged in great numerical strength. He reserved his fire until the King's Own were almost on him, and then opened up with everything he had. Lieutenant John Thompson approached an enemy machine gun nest which he covered with his pistol as

he called upon the crews to surrender. As they raised their hands, he lowered his pistol, but one of the Iraqis pressed the thumb piece of his gun and killed Thompson outright. Not one of the enemy left that place alive."

By 15:00 the Iraqis were in retreat, but they held up the advance of the King's Own at a ridge beyond the village. Dunford Wood continued:

"The King's Own attack and are held up at 'Hell Fire Corner', the ridge above Dhibban. Dan Cremin and his boys (minus me) go and shoot it up, and they all come back riddled with holes. I get up eventually with 'Tiny' Irwin in the back and machine gun the fleeing troops. They stop and shoot me up, but it seems slaughter all the same. Three Iraqi armoured cars come up, my bombs miss but Dan opens them up like a tin opener with a stick right down the road. Tony warns me they 'bite' so I don't go too low." [3]

The King's Own had lost five men and five wounded, but they came away with 435 Iraqi prisoners. As they returned to the camp, the bulk of the Iraqi forces were in full flight towards Fallujah.

In the afternoon, the Iraqi Air Force unexpectedly launched a heavy attack on the airfield and the polo ground. Dunford Wood recorded the attack in his diary:

"Northrops come over while I am eating lunch in the tent at 3.30 and drop bombs right across the polo ground and get one of our 'recco' Audaxes. The fire spreads to a Gladiator. Dicky Cleaver and Bob May wounded and some killed. They also riddle our tent with bullet holes."

Then a second heavy raid of Iraqi planes streaked over the camp at 17:00, and Dudgeon's observer was killed while loading bombs onto his Oxford.

> *"When I got back to my Oxford," Dudgeon wrote, "Arthur Prickett was lying on the ground underneath it, on his side with his knees bent up to his stomach. Five out of eight bombs had been loaded; three were still lying on the ground. I remember noting that the engines were still running. I crawled below the fuselage and rolled him onto his back. His eyes were open and his face had that particular yellow-blue tint which appears in seconds when the blood stops flowing. By this stage in the war it told me precisely what I was looking at. One more friend and colleague had gone from my life."*

In all, the two raids had cost two Oxfords, a Gladiator, and an Audax, along with seven killed and eight wounded. What Prickett had been preparing for, however, was a new attack on the fleeing Iraqis. Because at about 16:00, a large column of reinforcements was spotted on the road from Fallujah, and there was soon a chaotic traffic jam, as the retreating troops met the reinforcing column on the road in complete disorder. It was too good an opportunity to miss. Savile ordered every available aircraft of the Air Striking Force into the air. As Dunford Wood returned from the first raid on the ridge, his fellow Musketeer Pringle was preparing to take off:

> *"A convoy approaches from Fallujah and the boys go off, including Ian (Pringle), it being his turn. As he is buckling on his parachute I say to myself 'he won't come back', and sure enough he doesn't. He does several trips and then Alan (Haig) and I go up. Both sections*

of the convoy are in flames, between 'Canal Turn' and Fallujah, and I put some bombs on the road and a good burst with my front gun. Two trips I do, and on the second I bend one bombing quadrant and am unable to even use the other, it being so stiff. So I use the front gun and return home, during another raid at about 6.00pm. Some funny holes on the polo ground, like aerial torpedoes, and they were obviously aiming for our line of tents. They must reckon 'C' Squadron the most dangerous one! Well, Stonhill sees a plane dive into the ground near the convoy at about 6.15, and it turns out to be Ian and Fairweather in the back. But his bombs blew up, so he wouldn't have known much! What's the use. Hooray for the next man to die - Alan Haig or me." [4]

The Four Musketeers were now down to two.

The bombing of the column was relentless, and went on for about two hours. All that remained afterwards was a 250 yard strip of flames from wrecked and burning trucks, with intermittent exploding ammunition. In all, the Air Striking Force carried out 139 sorties that day, the majority in the attack on the convoy, for the loss of the one Audax piloted by Ian Pringle. Mornington Wentworth was ordered out the next morning to assess the damage:

"I didn't realise what had happened until the next morning, when I was sent out in an armoured car, as escort to the King's Own, to clear up the mess. And what a mess! Not one of those convoys reached us. There were vehicles in the wadis, either side of the road, hardly any in one piece, they'd set fire to them; there were dead bodies. After that, we never had any fears that the Iraqis would get through." [5]

Dunford Wood's aerial photographs on a reconnaissance flight told the same story. Further patrols of the Levies went up onto the Plateau, and confirmed that it was now completely empty of Iraqi troops. The five day siege was over.

For the next few days, the Levies and the Armoured Car Company were kept busy salvaging war materiel from the wreckage, which was spread far and wide across the Plateau as well as on the road to Fallujah. The booty was considerable - six Czech 3.7 inch howitzers with 2,400 shells, an eighteen pounder gun, an Italian tank, ten Crossley Armoured cars, seventy-nine trucks, three anti-aircraft guns with shells, and numerous Bren guns, Vickers heavy machine guns, rifles and ammunition. These were modern British weapons and ironically much more up to date than the ancient World War One era Lewis and Hotchkiss machine guns that British forces in Iraq and Palestine were equipped with. At a stroke, the firepower of Colonel Roberts' hotch-potch Habbaniya army was multiplied several fold. Dunford Wood recorded a trip to the Depot to look at it all:

> *"I go down to view all the booty and get myself an 18 lb shell case. There are all the guns and armoured cars and a wicked little Italian 'whippet' tank. I get myself issued with an Iraqi .38 at the depot by saying I haven't got a gun, so it can't really be classified as 'loot' or 'booty.'"*

Habbaniya's defenders had achieved an incredible victory. Through their bold and relentless action against overwhelming odds, unleashed by Smart at dawn on the 2nd May, within five days they had swept the enemy from a seemingly unassailable position Dudgeon wrote that in those five hectic days:

> *"Our hastily armed, outdated training machines had dropped well over three thousand bombs, totalling*

> *over fifty tons, and we had fired 116,000 rounds*
> *of ammunition. The Ops room had recorded 647*
> *sorties, but we had completed, unrecorded, many more*
> *than that...(because) a lot of the Audax pilots never*
> *bothered to spend time and energy walking a half*
> *mile from the Polo Pitch to the Ops room, just to tell*
> *the Butcher what they had done; they just got on with*
> *the job... Our losses were thirteen killed and twenty-*
> *one too wounded to carry on, and four more grounded*
> *from nerves gone."* [6]

However the Iraqis, had they chosen to, could have walked into the camp any day, or night, they chose. And yet they didn't. It's instructive to try to understand why.

On questioning Iraqi prisoners afterwards, it was clear that some of them had not eaten for two days, and that their water had run out. Many had ammunition pouches stuffed with dates to keep them going. Second, none of them had been briefed about what their real mission was, and to a man they believed they were on the Plateau for a training exercise. Many years later, Dudgeon made contact with the Iraqi who had been commanding one of the Iraqi fighter squadrons, whose Italian-built Bredas were more powerful than anything Habbaniya had until the arrival of the Blenheims. Air Colonel Hafdhi Aziz had been trained at RAF Cranwell in England, and was one of the five founding pilots of the Iraqi Air Force. He wrote to Dudgeon:

> *"Whatever happened in May 1941, we did not declare*
> *war. I want to know why the RAF came and bombed*
> *our air force without any warning early on Friday*
> *2nd May? And also they bombed our troops who were*
> *camping south of Habbaniya. You know, Friday is our*
> *Sunday, and every one of us was fast asleep in his bed."*

It seems that Rashid Ali's move against the British had been started in such haste that no joined-up plan had been put together. Their army and air force were totally unprepared. None of the four Colonels were noted for their military acumen, there was no central command and control. Each was responsible for their own particular division and region, and more concerned with their political careers than anything else. Meanwhile the political leadership - Rashid Ali and the Red Fox - were simply hoping the British would capitulate and sue for peace. Such as it was, their 'grand strategy' was to spin out negotiations long enough for the promised German help to arrive.

As for the ensuing fight, Iraqi, Egyptian and Syrian soldiers in World War Two were notorious for buckling under air bombardment. Whether this was understood at the time by the senior commanders at Habbaniya is unclear, but after the war General Hellmuth Felmy, who was to organise the Luftwaffe contingent that was sent to Iraq in the coming days, and was later to be involved in raising an Arab battalion to fight for the Nazis, noted:

> "In battle these units usually fail to stand up to heavy
> artillery fire, armoured attacks and air raids. To a
> certain extent this weakness can be overcome by combat
> training. However, even then an unforeseen situation
> might lead to panic."

Lastly, there was still a good deal of respect for the power of the British, especially amongst ordinary soldiers, despite their reverses against the Nazis. If they had sniffed any sign of defeatism or vacillation amongst the defenders of Habbaniya, the outcome would have been very different. But the fury of the attack both took them by surprise and cowed them into submission. The introduction of the two ancient howitzers on May 4th took the bombardment to a new level, appearing as it did to the Iraqis that the British were being reinforced with artillery. Unprepared as they were, with limited food supplies, no comforts and no clear understanding of why they were there, surrounded by an ever-mounting death toll under the relentless bombardment, they fled.

§

But the embassy staff fifty miles away in Baghdad knew nothing of this. They were still unsure about what was happening. During the 5th and 6th a gloom had descended. In the late afternoon of the 5th an unsettling message was broadcast by London that the British Government would be prepared to negotiate with Rashid Ali if he withdrew his forces, an offer that was repeated by a Palestinian radio station.

On the 6th, Baghdad radio was claiming that the British were suing for peace. Then, on the 7th, just as everyone in the embassy was gathering in the ballroom to hear the evening update from Dr Sindersen, the Scottish royal physician, machine guns started up from the roofs of neighbouring buildings and everyone scrambled for cover under tables and chairs. Freya Stark remembers a 'huge roar', as a "Gladiator came swooping almost to touch the palm trees on the lawn and drop a letter from Habbaniya." It turned out to be an Audax piloted by 'C' Squadron's Pilot Officer Garner. News of the safe evacuation of the women and children, and the lifting of the siege, brought instant celebration.

That same evening Churchill cabled Smart, unaware that he had retired hurt:

> *"Your vigorous and splendid action has largely restored the situation. We are watching the grand fight you are making. All possible aid will be sent."*

Because it was not over yet. Although they could now sleep well at night, and the main aerodrome could be used safely, the

*Churchill's message was distributed around the camp on
8th May in issue 4 of the Daily Bulletin.*

hangars buzzing with repairs, there was still the occasional attack
by the Iraqi Air Force. On the 8th Dunford Wood wrote:

> *"A bit of tip-and-run bombing from 'Peggy' Audaxes
> (yesterday), one of which is shot down by a Blenheim
> fighter. A Savoia and a Northrop spotted force landed
> in the desert, and are destroyed after a prodigious
> amount of bombs, S.A.A (small arms ammunition)
> and Very lights have been used on them. Dan Cremin,
> returning from the furthermost one, meets a 'Peggy'
> Audax going home, but as his front gun had jammed,
> he does nothing. But the two planes on the ground are
> at 065 degrees. so when this is plotted on the map it
> leads to Baquba. Yesterday afternoon they bomb it,
> Stonhill, Broadhurst, Haig and Frewin..."*[7]

The camp's daily bulletin No. 3, issued on the 8th, explained
the significance of this attack:

"Yesterday, the 7th, saw the virtual elimination from the war of the majority of the remaining aircraft of the Iraqi air force. We had long been searching for the satellite landing ground concealing the balance of their striking force. All likely places had been explored, but only blanks drawn. Then in the early afternoon, the report came back: twenty-one Iraqi aircraft were on the ground at Baquba about 30 miles N.E.E. of Baghdad. Immediately our aircraft went into action, bombing and machine gunning. At least three enemy machines were set on fire and the remainder almost certainly damaged beyond immediate repair."

The report makes no mention of Stonhill being shot down and captured, but it is clear that the Iraqi Air Force is no longer effective as a fighting force.

However, despite the loss of their air force, the Iraqis still had two Brigades dug in nearby, one at Ramadi and one at Fallujah, and a division not far away in Baghdad - though ironically, in breaking the bunds and flooding large areas of desert around Habbaniya, the Iraqis made it just as hard for them to re-approach Habbaniya as it was for the forces in Habbaniya, or Basrah, to approach Baghdad. It was a defensive move, to await the help that was expected any day from Germany. Habbaniya, despite being out of immediate danger, was still in a very uncomfortable situation.

So what of the 'all possible aid' that Churchill was referring to?

~

1. Habbaniya Daily Bulletin No. 3, 7th May 1941.
2. In Every Place: The RAF Cars in the Middle East, Nigel Warwick, page 284.
3 .The War Diaries of Colin Dunford Wood, Vol 1, 6th May 1941.
4. The War Diaries of Colin Dunford Wood, Vol 1, 6th May 1941.
5. In Every Place: The RAF Cars in the Middle East, Nigel Warwick, p286.
6. The War That Never Was, Tony Dudgeon, p120.
7. The War Diaries of Colin Dunford Wood, Vol 1, 8th May 1941.

Part 3

An Arab Legion armoured car.

Habforce

A FEW DAYS EARLIER, ON THE 4TH, a rumour had circulated in the camp. Dunford Wood recorded that *"a mechanised column took Rutbah and reached 'H4' landing ground on the pipeline yesterday. Hope they get here before the Germans do."* The same rumour was reported by Freya Stark holed up in the embassy, about the same time.

The rumour was partially true. Rutbah Wells, eight-five miles short of the Transjordanian border, had served as an Imperial Airways layover stop, with a rest house in the old fort.[1] On May 2nd, Iraqi desert police, who had occupied the Rutbah fort a few days earlier, had fired on British contractors, and it seemed likely that Iraqi reinforcements would soon arrive in greater numbers to guard this route from the west. So the next day a small British led force was formed at the H4 pumping station on the Kirkuk-

Haifa pipeline, on the Transjordan side of the border. This was the 'mechanised column' Dunford Wood was referring to, made up of a squadron of the Transjordanian border force, an Imperial force of Arab soldiers with British officers.

Their principal objective was to occupy the landing strips at the pumping stations, as news was starting to reach the British of preparations to move German aircraft to Syria, and if the Germans were able to capture these landing grounds, they would have made good bases from which to advance towards Habbaniya. However, though the Transjordan Border Force moved across the border the next day and occupied the pumping station at H3, some thirty-five miles short of Rutbah Wells, they refused to go any further, claiming that their terms of service did not allow them to fight other than in defence of Transjordan. In reality, they baulked at the possibility that they would have to fire on fellow Arabs.

Back in Palestine, the more substantial help that had for so long been demanded by Churchill was slowly getting into gear, in spite of Wavell's opinion that it would be too late to relieve Habbaniya. On 6th May, Major General George Clark, the military commander of Palestine and GOC of the 1st Cavalry Division which was stationed there, was tasked with assembling a column. This was to be called 'Habforce'.

The forces he had available were meagre, given that Palestine had earlier been stripped to supply troops for both Greece and to face Rommel in Libya - a fact that Wavell had already pointed out to the Chiefs of Staff. The bulk of the relief column was to be made up of the Household Cavalry of the 4th Cavalry Brigade, commanded by Brigadier Joe Kingstone. This illustrious unit had recently been converted from horses to trucks, so in effect had been ignominiously demoted to the role of mobile infantry, a fact they were not at all happy about. They had also been forced to shoot many of their horses, as well as leave their pack of hounds behind.[2]

The other component of the 4th Cavalry Brigade, the Royal Wiltshire Yeomanry, were just then in North Africa, so were hastily recalled. Their role would be to guard the lines of communication as Habforce marched across the desert, and they too had recently converted from horses to trucks. Both these forces had had little time to acclimatise to their new 'mechanised' role and were sorely short of equipment.[3] Above all, few of these troops had traversed a desert before, let alone fought in one, and they were now being asked to cross 500 miles of sand in a dash to Habbaniya.

In addition, the RAF's No 2 Armoured Car Company was also recalled from the Western desert to join Habforce with its eight Fordson armoured cars, together with 237 Battery of the Royal Artillery, recently arrived at Suez from the UK, an anti-tank troop of the Royal Artillery, a troop of Royal Engineers, and a detachment of field ambulances. Last, Habforce was to include 350 men of Transjordan's Arab Legion under Major John Bagot Glubb - 'Glubb Pasha' - an independent force in Ford pick-up trucks equipped with World War One era Lewis and Hotchkiss machine guns. Glubb's official role was as the column's Political Officer, with a mission to encourage the tribes, with whom he was familiar from his time with the British Army in Iraq in the 1920s, to rise up in support of the deposed Regent. His force was not part of the British command structure, unlike the imperial Transjordan Frontier Force which was led by British officers and served as part of the British Forces in the Middle East, but was raised by and paid for by the Emir of Transjordan himself. However, as the brother of the deposed Regent, the Emir was more than happy to loan them to Habforce for this mission and as an escort for Glubb. Glubb himself was a kind of latter day Lawrence of Arabia,[4] and his presence as a semi-independent operator with Habforce was to cause some confusion to the British army officers who were tasked with the mission.

This mission was daunting. As Captain Somerset de Chair, a sitting M.P. and the intelligence officer attached to Habforce, wrote soon afterwards, this 'motley army' had to march from *'the shores of the Mediterranean to the Euphrates across a tract of waterless desert never before in all history crossed by a conquering army.'*[5] According to all the military textbooks, it was impossible to capture Baghdad from the West.

From the railhead at Mafraq in Transjordan, the distance to Habbaniya was about 470 miles. For the first 170 miles, past the H4 pumping station to the border, the way was tarmaced, but this petered out just a few miles into Iraq. From there to Ramadi, via H3 and Rutbah Wells, a distance of 280 miles to just short of Habbaniya, the traveller was forced to choose from a maze of desert tracks on undulating stone and sand, man-made and animal made, long stretches of which were constantly shifting with sandstorms. The only way to navigate this wilderness was with a compass bearing and with the help of the stars. Long stretches of soft sand lay in wait for the unwary, and only a handful of the army's vehicles were tracked. In fact many had to be requisitioned from the streets of Jerusalem and Haifa - including municipal buses with their civilian drivers - while the Household Cavalry had to travel in Morris commercial trucks.

In addition to the risks of direction finding, and navigating around soft sand obstacles, there was no fuel en-route and precious few water resources. Rutbah Wells was about the only place with wells where water could easily be obtained, and it was vulnerable to sabotage by the Iraqis. So the troops had to carry enough fuel and water to get them across the desert, and there was little to spare should they get lost or stuck. Flatbed trucks were requisitioned to carry one gallon of water per man per day plus one gallon per vehicle per day, as well as rations to last seven days. Much of the water came in petrol cans from Egypt and varied in colour from purple to black - it had to be settled for ten minutes to drain the sediment before it could be drunk. And it was warm or sometimes even hot, depending on the time of day.

On May 6th Wavell cabled Dill, the CIGS, in London:

"Concentration of Habforce for relief of Habbaniya

proceeding as rapidly as possible. Have ordered
immediate occupation of Rutbah to be attempted, it
seems to be only lightly held. Situation at Habbaniya
apparently stable and signs that enemy may be short of
gun ammunition and waiting Axis aid..." [6]

As we have seen, the first attempt on Rutbah had failed. On hearing that the advance party of the Transjordan Frontier Force had refused to attack the Fort, Major General Clark ordered them to return to H3 and be disarmed. It did not bode well, considering a considerable part of Habforce was made up of Arab troops. In their place, he ordered the more reliable Arab Legion under Glubb, who were already in the area, to make an attempt, and arranged for a small flight of four Blenheims to be sent to the H4 landing ground in support.

Later that day news of the lifting of the siege reached Wavell - surprisingly not from Habbaniya itself, which was still engaged in the battle for Sin el Dhibban, nor from the embassy in Baghdad, which remained incommunicado, but from an intercept in London of an Italian message which reported that the Iraqis had exhausted their supply of bombs and ammunition and requested that German aircraft support be accelerated. It was clear from this message that German help was on its way. So Wavell messaged the Chiefs of Staff for new instructions, since his original objective, the relief of Habbaniya, seemed to have been overtaken by events.

"Now that the Iraqi force appears to have withdrawn
from Habbaniya, require urgently guide to policy.
Is RAF to continue attacking military objectives
throughout Iraq? Have no knowledge of situation
Baghdad, is Rashid's Government still in power and
is there any sign of change of attitude? Habforce will
advance to Habbaniya as soon as assembled, H3
already in our hands." [7]

In reality their departure was still a number of days away. Clark had to assemble forces from all over Palestine and Egypt. Given the urgency, he decided to split the column in two. Up front and travelling in the fastest vehicles would be a flying column under Brigadier Kingstone, to be named Kingcol, which would include the armoured cars, the Household Cavalry, the two Royal artillery units, and an additional force brought up from internal security duties in Haifa - two companies of the Essex Regiment. Their mission was to rendezvous with Glubb's Arab Legion, which it was hoped would have secured Rutbah before they arrived. Behind them would come the bulk of the force, and the whole lot would meet up at Habbaniya within a week.

So while preparations were made for the column's departure, Glubb moved off from H4 towards the Iraqi border on 9th May. When he reached Rutbah, his force threw a cordon around the fort - thought to contain about one hundred Iraqi police - while they waited for the Blenheims to bomb them into submission. Eventually four long range Blenheims from 203 Squadron operating from Kibrit on the Suez Canal arrived to bomb the fort, but most of the bombs landed harmlessly in the desert and the attack proved inconclusive. The Iraqis showed no signs of surrendering, and one of the Blenheims was badly damaged by small arms fire and crashed on the return journey. Glubb's force waited patiently for a second day, unable to make a frontal attack on the fort with just the small arms they had, but trying to persuade the Iraqis to give up. However, that evening an Iraqi relief column was spotted advancing in pick-up trucks from the north, so Glubb ordered a retreat to H3, preferring to wait for the bigger force coming up behind him. The Iraqi press had a field day, claiming a great victory at Rutbah, and that Glubb had been killed - news that was repeated by the BBC and in the British press.

The next day the 2nd Armoured Car Company, under Squadron Leader Casano, were sent ahead to reinforce him. Incredibly, they had only left Sidi Barrani in Egypt a few days before, and had travelled almost continuously for 1,100 miles. This time they had more luck. On approaching the fort, the armoured cars fought a fierce engagement with the recently arrived Iraqi force,[8] and after six hours of intermittent fighting, the Iraqis retreated. That night a Valentia from Shaibah bombed the fort, and when Casano arrived back to have another crack at the fort in the morning, he spotted the huge wooden gates of the fort ajar. Gingerly his armoured cars approached. The place was deserted - the Iraqis had gone.

Finally, on the 11th, all the remaining elements of Habforce were assembled on the Palestinian coast at Netanya and ready to leave, Kingcol in front. In all, the column stretched for seven miles. Kingcol itself consisted of 2,000 troops and five hundred vehicles, and carried four days ration of water, and five days supply of fuel. There was no margin for error.

The same day, Wavell flew to Jerusalem for a final conference with General Wilson and Air Vice-Marshal d'Albiac, who was preparing to replace the evacuated Smart as AOC of Habbaniya. Both had recently returned from the abortive campaign in Greece. With Habforce's commander, Major General Clark, they pored over the maps as they made final checks on the plan, for it had been made clear to Wavell by London that they would be expected to continue to Baghdad and overthrow Rashid Ali now that Habbaniya was safe. No one was under any illusion as to the scale of the task, considering the limited force they had and the challenge of the journey over the desert. They did not even have a single tank. Wavell's parting words to Clark were only mildly encouraging: *'It's a long odds bet, but I think you will make it.'*

Habforce spent their first night just north of Amman at Mafraq, digging-in a large square in the desert against air attack, with the Royal Artillery units guarding the perimeter and the remaining armoured cars - those not ahead with Casano - on picket duty out in the desert.

James Glass, an RASC driver, recalled the scene:

157

"Our camping arrangements were interesting. We went into 'laager' - as the Roman Legions and as North American settlers did. We drove round into a huge square, two deep. In the centre we settled the ambulances and Field Hospital, also the HQ and Signals. The Signals busied themselves putting up the aerials and transmitters, and setting up the connections. The Field Artillery on the perimeter turned their 25 lb guns round facing outwards at the ready. Then the little scout cars went out, about a mile - we could see them with their flares at the ready in case of surprise attacks. At this stage, no attack was expected, but practice was essential." [9]

On the 12th, they reached H4. The next day Kingcol's commander, Brigadier Kingstone, accompanied by his Intelligence officer, Captain de Chair, went ahead with a company of the Household Cavalry and reached Rutbah by evening.

They were relieved to find the wells had not been spiked by the departing Iraqis. It was the first time any of them had met Glubb, and de Chair recorded the meeting with amusement. Glubb appeared in the candlelit gloom of the Beau Geste style fort in the middle of the desert with *"a yellow keffiyah fastened to his head by the double ropes of a black silk aqal"* and a little sandy moustache. He had many ribbons on his tunic and, on his shoulder tabs, *"crossed swords and two stars of a peculiar design which Joe Kingstone had never seen before."* [10] De Chair recorded Kingstone's initial impressions:

> *"'This fellow thinks he is King of Saudi Arabia,' said Kingstone afterwards, 'The trouble is that I don't know whether he is senior to me or not.' They were like two prima donnas billed to perform in the same opera."*

At 04:00 the next morning, the 14th, the rest of Kingcol arrived, while the bulk of Habforce stayed behind at H4 to await news from the flying column that it was safe to proceed. Kingcol remained at Rutbah for the next day, busying themselves with stocking up with water for the last, and most dangerous two hundred mile stretch of waterless desert to Habbaniya. It wasn't long before Habbaniya made contact. Dudgeon arrived in the morning in a Blenheim with news that a German Heinkel had been spotted on a bombing raid over Hinaidi air base, while an Audax on reconnaissance over Mosul had been fired on by an ME110. It seemed scarcely credible. But as if to confirm the presence of the Luftwaffe, de Chair received a report over the radio from Palestine that seven unidentified aircraft had been spotted flying over Beirut headed for Iraq, while German planes had been seen at Damascus and Palmyra. In fact, late that afternoon permission was given by Major General Clark for an attack to be made on the airfield at Palmyra, the first time on Syria soil and a virtual declaration of war on Vichy France. Two of the new American built Curtiss Tomahawks fighters from Egypt escorting three Blenheims staged through H4 on their way to Palmyra, where they just missed three Heinkels which had left for Mosul, but they damaged at least one further Heinkel and a couple of JU90 transport planes still on the ground. Further attacks were made on Damascus and Palmyra airfields the next day.

It appeared that, very late in the day, the Germans were finally swinging into action. As de Chair noted, *"it looked rather as if we were for it."* [11] Dunford Wood had echoed the same sentiment the evening before in his diary: *"A few Heinkels reported by the British minister at Beirut, and the Turkish consul at Mosul. Russia has recognised Rashid Ali, so what to do? This isn't over yet."*

The curtain was about to rise on the final act of the opera.

~

1. One traveller described it as an "unforgettable experience of arriving at the most desolate and extraordinary hostelry in the world".

2. The Household Cavalry were made up of the two most senior regiments in the army, the Blues and Royals and the Life Guards, who guarded the monarch in peacetime. Their officers came from the aristocracy and the landed gentry, and they liked to hunt to hounds regardless of where they were in the world. Losing their horses and being put into trucks was quite a shock.

3. The 1st Cavalry Division that garrisoned Palestine had been stripped of their artillery, engineers, signals, and most of their transport to provide for the needs of other formations in Greece, North Africa, and East Africa.

4. Glubb went on after the war to serve the Emir and then King of Jordan, Hussein, as commander of the Jordanian army.

5. The Golden Carpet, Somerset de Chair, p15.

6. Wavell, John Connell, p440.

7. Wavell, John Connell, p440.

8. A force of 500 irregulars under Arab guerrilla leader Fawzi al-Qawuqji, a ruthless fighter who did not hesitate to murder or mutilate prisoners. He was a follower of the Red Fox and had come with him from Syria.

9. A Reminiscence of War 1939-1945, James Glass, p6.

10. The Golden Carpet, Somerset de Chair.

11. The Golden Carpet, Somerset de Chair, p 21.

ME110s of Fliegerfuhrer Irak being prepared in the Balkans.

The Luftwaffe Arrives

FOLLOWING THE FRENETIC EVENTS of early May, the tempo of life at Habbaniya had reduced somewhat. Since the 8th the Iraqi air force had all but disappeared, and there was breathing space to repair the planes and tend to more mundane matters. On the 12th Dunford Wood reported:

> *"Alan and I do Pete (Gillespy) and Ian's (Pringle) things the other day, packing them up etc, and a more depressing job I never had. We sort of give them each a dressing gown (no idea whose is whose) and share out the shoes evenly. I collect all Pete's mess bills and give them to the adjutant who will have some fun sorting them out."* [1]

161

But as reports of German activity start to filter through, the tension cranks up again. On the 15th he reports:

> *"A Blenheim is attacked four times by an ME110 at Mosul and six ME109s are seen nearby in Northern Iraq.[2] I go off to drop leaflets on Fallujah, which requires no small skill, and the prisoners' mail, addressed to the postmaster there. Then last night I go up solo, 2.15 to 4.30, half asleep all the time, and having nothing to do but think of MEs landing by moonlight and the first light of dawn."[3]*

As Dunford Wood was imagining Messerschmitts landing by moonlight, Kingcol was starting to move out of Rutbah, the Household Cavalry up front as an advance guard, accompanied by a truckload of 'Glubb's Girls' - which was the nickname given to the Arab Legion by the British on account of their flowing robes - as guides. Speed and density, key considerations for any military advance across open ground without air cover, was set at fifteen miles an hour and twenty vehicles to the mile. De Chair was in charge of navigation, and with the aid of a compass, he followed the route of the new Haifa-Bagdad road, yet to be constructed but marked every few miles by small cairns of piled up stones. To the north, at Ramadi, lay a brigade of the Iraqi army, and they had blown the culverts that traversed the flooded area on the main road to Habbaniya, to prevent the approach from Rutbah. To reach the camp, Colonel Roberts messaged instructions from Habbaniya that the column should branch south at a point called Kilo 25, and take a detour around the south of Habbaniya lake across a further stretch of desert to the village of Mujara. The King's Own had occupied the village on May 10th, Dunford Wood acting as air support in an Audax, and since then the Royal Engineers had been feverishly building a trestle bridge to enable Kingcol to cross the water regulator of the Mujara canal. They all knew that if this bridge was found and bombed by the Germans, Kingcol would not be able to reach Habbaniya at all, and would be caught in the open.

As the last vehicle moved out of Rutbah, the leaders were twenty miles ahead. James Glass, driving a truckload of Essex infantrymen, recalled the scene years later:

> "We used old tracks; there were no roads. Sometimes we had smooth hard sand, sometimes soft sand that we sank in. We would also come across acres and acres of large boulders and we had to find the best way through - we would lose our sense of direction. The mileage travelled per day varied hugely. Lots of drivers couldn't read the surface and so many got bogged down, and it was out with the sand tracks, ropes, spades, etc and get the b-----s out. We couldn't leave any of the vehicles. They were all necessary... I should say here that the tracks through the desert were lined with dead animals, decomposing fast, and bleached bones - indeed whole skeletons. There had been no military engagements so there were no human remains. Of course, we knew that we would have to bury bodies immediately, if death occurred for any reason." [4]

Early in the afternoon, a lone Heinkel appeared. At the same time, two British Gladiators, one piloted by Dudgeon, were on a reconnaissance trip to check on the progress of the column. Amazingly, neither the Heinkel nor the Gladiators spotted each other, and after the Heinkel dropped a couple of bombs on the stragglers and machine-gunned one of the Essex trucks, it pushed off back to Mosul. Luckily there were no fatalities. But Kingcol had been discovered at last.

§

The Heinkel that had found them had flown from Mosul, four hundred miles to the north. The Lufwaffe commander, Colonel Junck, had only arrived that morning from Syria. It had been a long journey. His unit - *Fliegerführer Irak* - was part of a larger combined service force known as *Special Staff F (Sonderstab F)*, which had been formed by the German High Command after Hitler had finally given Ribbentrop the green light on May 3rd. General Hellmuth Felmy, based in Greece, was put in overall command. The plan was to bring it up to strength with three elements - Junck's Luftwaffe force, *Fliegerführer Irak*, a Foreign Ministry delegation under Fritz Grobba, travelling under the pseudonym "Franz Gehrke", and finally, within the next few weeks, a Brandenburger regiment of commandos. A small group of Brandenburger special forces were included in the first wave with Grobba, who had been the first to arrive in Iraq on the 10th, having flown out via Rhodes and Aleppo with two Heinkels and two ME 110s.

About the same time, Ambassador Rahn[5] was beginning to organise arms supplies from Syria - the first shipment of which had arrived in Mosul via train from Aleppo a few days previously.

Unlike the pilots he was to command, Junck had had some experience of serving in the tropics, but even so, the logistical challenge of the mission was daunting. From a standing start on 6th May, when Luftwaffe chief Goring had given him his orders in Berlin, he had had to coordinate logistics and supplies for a scratch force of two Luftwaffe squadrons, adapt them for action in desert conditions, and then transport their support staff, spares and equipment over 1,000 miles in radio silence to a battle theatre where intelligence was scarce. In addition to providing for these stores and equipment, he would also need to take into account the much lower grade aviation fuel available in Iraq. It might be good enough for 1930s biplanes, but it would certainly cause problems for the more modern German machines.

Thirteen JU52 and the larger JU90 transport aircraft were provided to transport supplies and ground crews, and one was kitted out as a flying chemical laboratory and mini-oil refinery, enabling the force to adulterate the local fuel in situ to make it usable.

However, Grobba insisted on taking space for his public relations and intelligence staff, along with their office equipment - in fact he planned a fully equipped diplomatic mission. Junck was also told that all but three of the transport aircraft could make just a single trip. They would be needed back in Greece for the planned assault on Crete. So from the outset, his room for manoeuvre was severely squeezed.

The main force was made up of twelve Heinkel 111 medium bombers in an initial group of seven and then a further five, and fourteen Messerschmitt Bf 110 fighter-bombers.[6] Prior to flying out, the unit had prepared in Greece, the planes painted in Iraq Air Force colours and made ready for desert conditions, while a reconnaissance group under Major Axel Von Blomberg, the son of Field Marshal Blomberg, had gone ahead to make contact with the Iraqi Government and prepare for the main group's arrival.

So by the 11th, the day Habforce set off, the Germans already had two small detachments in the country - the diplomats and a couple of Brandenburgers with Grobba, and a Luftwaffe contingent under Von Blomberg, and it was one of their aircraft that was spotted by the British at Hinaidi air base. As soon as he had arrived, Grobba had hastened to Baghdad to meet Rashid Ali. In addition to the welcome moral support, he'd also brought gold and foreign currency - £10,000 in gold for Rashid Ali and $15,000 in banknotes for the Red Fox - with the promise of more to follow later in the month. They had agreed to meet again on the 16th to plan the military campaign, once Junck had arrived.

Junck had had an eventful journey. There had been a little local difficulty with the Vichy French, who had at first refused refuelling rights to his main force in Damascus - clearly Damascus and Paris were not communicating properly, and the provisions of the Paris protocols were not yet well understood on the ground. The local

Vichy authorities were nervous of giving the British any excuse for a bombing raid, and they wanted the German planes gone as soon as possible. Eventually the Germans were told that they needed to go on to Palmyra, one hundred and fifty miles away, where fuel and supplies would be provided. Unfortunately, due to the lack of space on the Junkers transport aircraft, the Heinkels had been loaded with additional spares and ammunition. The airstrip at Palmyra proved very rough, and the tail wheels of two of the bombers collapsed on landing. They had to be left behind for repairs, while the rest of the force departed on their last leg to Mosul. As chance would have it, three roving Blenheims from 203 Squadron found them on the ground the next day. It seemed that the fears of the Vichy French were well founded.

Junck arrived in Iraq on the morning of the 15th. It did not take long for him to realise the scale of the challenge that faced him. Though the British built accommodation was of a good standard, the facilities at Mosul air base were rudimentary - there were no anti-aircraft defences, no protected dispersal areas and worst of all, the additional petrol supplies they had been promised were even more unsuitable than he had been led to believe, several tanks containing petrol for cars. The chemical laboratory was immediately put to use creating the low octane aviation fuel that his planes needed to function properly, but it was a laborious task. Nor was his first sight of the Iraqi air force encouraging - it had almost entirely been wiped out, and the Iraqi personnel appeared sullen and defeated.

As a morale boost, he decided to send a lone Heinkel to try to locate Habforce in the desert, while he sent Von Blomberg, his liaison officer, ahead to Baghdad to make arrangements for the council of war with the Iraqi Government already planned for the 16th.

Von Blomberg set off in a Heinkel. When it landed at Hinaidi air base he was found dead in his seat. What exactly happened was never established. The Iraqi Government maintained that he was hit by a stray bullet from a tribesman, while a more likely scenario was that the plane was shot at by an Iraqi soldier guarding a bridge over the Euphrates, who did not recognise the unusual shape of the plane as it flew low over the city to boost Iraqi morale. Whatever the source of the bullet, it was a lucky shot and went straight through von Blomberg's neck - an inauspicious start to the mission.

Grobba was furious, and flew down to Baghdad the next day with Junck to meet Rashid Ali and his senior commanders. They agreed on a number of priorities for *Fliegerfuhrer Irak*. First, they must prevent Habforce reaching Habbaniya; second, the goal was the capture of Habbaniya itself, with *Fliegerfuhrer Irak* in support of the Iraqi army. The agreement concluded by highlighting one overriding objective - to provide *'spine stiffening for the Iraqis whose army had become terrified of bombing by British aircraft.'*

The same day, Junck ordered an attack on Habbaniya by three Heinkels and six ME100s. Dunford Wood recorded the events that evening:

> *"I have just taken off on a recco with Tiny (Irwin) and look back to see smoke over the camp, and three Heinkels high in the air. One is lagging behind, with a Gladiator on its tail. The Gladiator is then shot down and we see the pilot bail out. The parachute fails to open properly and we go low over his body and the plane, which had exploded in mid air.*
>
> *We return and report it, and see one Heinkel with smoke coming out of one engine. It isn't seen anymore. Most of the bombs fall on the supply depot. Then six MEs get Reggie Wall, but the story is a bit confused and he is in hospital, not dead thank God."*[7]

The next day, he filled in the story:

> *"Saw Reggie Wall, who has a lot of 'superficial' holes in him. He was testing a plane and doing a wide circuit when six ME110s caught him over Dhibban. He did a crash landing somewhere, got out and ran for shelter and they dropped a bomb near him. The ambulance, which had been collecting the body of young Herrtage, in that Gladiator, saw it and stopped for him, and was machine gunned by the Hun."* [8]

The testing was a wireless trial in preparation for air to ground communication in support of Habforce, once they arrived - something they had space to do, now that the Iraqi air force and the troops on the Plateau had gone. But there was a new and much more powerful foe in the skies. Wall was lucky to be alive.

Oberleutnant Reinhard Graubner, the pilot of the Heinkel that shot down Herrtage in the Gladiator, remembers the thrill of the Lutwaffe's first kill of the campaign:

> *"The fighter slowly climbed towards us. Soon it hung behind us, and we heard the clattering of machine gun fire - one could not tell whether it was our own, or the enemy fire hitting us. Prinz (his co-pilot) and I suddenly saw many hits appearing on both wings, accompanied by a murderous roaring noise. I heard from behind 'Shot down!', and could not believe it when Ofw Thomas, the flight engineer, reported 'Now it is breaking up - now it has crashed'. Our well aimed return fire had succeeded! The first incontestable victory of our Gruppe!"* [9]

Graubner's elation was short lived, however, as his Heinkel had also been hit, and within twenty minutes he had been forced to crash land en route back to Mosul.

The raid did a lot more damage than any of the previous attacks by the Iraqi air force. The Heinkels had made two passes, dropping six 4,400 lb bombs, and destroyed several hangars, killing a number of ground crew. Luckily the planes they destroyed on the ground were all being repaired, and not operational. A couple of Hurricanes that had arrived from Egypt the day before, unannounced, from Egypt, were unscathed.

The next day, the Habbaniya Air Striking Force were to get their revenge.

~

1. The War Diaries of Colin Dunford Wood, Vol 1, 12th May 1941.
2. This report was obviously false, because no ME109s were operating in Iraq. However, this rumour of them would have unnerved the British pilots because no plane they had was a match for the fast and nimble fighters. There were several reports of ME109s being seen at Mosul by British pilots in the following days, but they were most likely remnant monoplanes of the Iraqi air force. However, the reports were credible enough to be reported at a War Cabinet briefing in London on 15th May: *"On the 14th May, six monoplanes, believed to be Me. 109's, were seen at Erbil, fifty miles east of Mosul, and three Heinkel III's have also been reported."* The National Archives CAB 66/16/25
3. The War Diaries of Colin Dunford Wood, Vol 1, 15th May 1941.
4. A Reminiscence of War 1939-1945, James Glass, pp 5-6.
5. The German ambassador in Paris, who had negotiated the 'Paris Protocols' just days earlier with the Vichy government to transfer arms from Syria to Iraq, and who had arrived in Damascus to direct the operation.
6. These were part of a unit, ZG 76, known as the 'Shark Group' (Haifischgruppe) due to their distinct shark's teeth nose decoration, meant to strike fear into their opponents. See Dust Clouds p 180 for details of this force.
7. The War Diaries of Colin Dunford Wood, Vol 1, 16th May 1941.
8. The War Diaries of Colin Dunford Wood, Vol 1, 17th May 1941.
9. Dust Clouds in the Middle East, Christopher Shores, p186.

*Elements of Kingcol in the desert on the approach to Habbaniya,
being shadowed by an aircraft from the camp.*

The Phantom Column

DESPITE THE LOSS OF THE AIRCRAFT and the casualties
at Habbaniya, it was perhaps fortunate for the British that
Fliegerfuhrer Irak concentrated their attention on Habbaniya
instead of Kingcol that day - because Kingcol were in trouble.
Having left Rutbah at dawn the previous day, they had eventually
reached the beginning of the tarmac road that led to Ramadi in the
late afternoon - though not without incident, as some miles short
of the tarmac they had encountered a heart-stopping short stretch
of soft sand which they had to rush in order to get across. They

bivouacked off the road, spread out over several square miles, just short of a spot on the map called Kilo 25, which was marked by a rusty iron plate on a pole. They were now within striking distance of Habbaniya. However, between them and the camp lay miles of floods engineered by the Iraqi army, as well as a brigade of their troops dug in at Ramadi. This was the point at which Colonel Roberts had said they should strike south off the road and head around the bottom of Lake Habbaniya, towards the Mujara canal, where the recently constructed trestle bridge was waiting to take them across and up to the camp from the south. But they would need to be quick, because it would not be long before the Germans discovered it, and then the route would be blocked.

That evening Kingstone and his commanders held a Brigade conference in the signal truck and made a plan for the following day. De Chair was to station his vehicle at the Kilo 25 sign, and point the trucks on a compass bearing that would take them to a wadi from where the Mujara canal was directly east. As de Chair wrote later: *"How little we realised what the day was to mean, as Henry (Abel-Smith) and I sat light-heartedly on a cairn of stones, watching the vehicles turn off into the desert."* [1] They were like two gamekeepers directing guests on a grouse moor in Scotland.

The next morning the column started as planned, and one by one the trucks left the road and headed off across the desert in a south easterly direction. Glubb's force had been ordered to go on reconnaissance to protect the flanks of the column, so he was not there to witness what happened next. As he later remarked, the British army has a fatal inclination to rely on a compass bearing alone when navigating deserts, with little regard to varied conditions of the desert floor. Going across a long stretch of sand in a straight line will invariably lead to disaster, which is what happened before long to the first of the three ton trucks to hit a patch of soft sand. Moreover, in order to protect against air attack, they were instructed to fan out, which meant that there were multiple opportunities for vehicles to get into difficulty. Soon large sections

172

of the column had come to a complete halt, as one vehicle tried to tow out its neighbour, and before long, troops were lounging around in 120-degree heat, the metal of their vehicles too hot to touch, while others laboured to dig theirs out from the treacherous dunes. It was the hottest recorded weather in twenty-five years, and to add further to their discomfort, a blistering *Khamsin* [2] blew sand and dust for long stretches of the day. If the Luftwaffe had chosen this moment to strafe the column, Kingcol was a sitting duck.

After several hours, a despairing Brigadier Kingstone ordered all vehicles that were not stuck to return to Kilo 25. All but two trucks limped back, and they set up camp again, burnt, exhausted and demoralised. They had enough water for thirty-six hours, but if they failed to find a new route the following day, Kingstone knew he would be forced to order their return to Rutbah.

So on the 17th, while the column rested in their makeshift camp at Kilo 25, Glubb's force went off with the Brigadier to scout an alternative route, and eventually they managed to navigate around the treacherous dunes in a wide loop, starting due south and then swinging around to reach the bridge at Mujara. While Kingstone went ahead to Habbaniya to report progress, Glubb retraced the route to Kilo 25. Kingstone returned that evening in a Blenheim, and they all set off again the next morning in single file, careful to follow the tracks of the Arab drivers at the head of the column.

This time the Germans found them, and four ME110s from Mosul strafed the tail end of the column as it was pulling out of the camp in mid-morning, killing one of Glubb's men and wounding several others, as well as some of the Household Cavalry. However, fortunately the direction they were headed was due south, so it looked as if they were headed away from Habbaniya and certainly not headed for Mujara. If the planes had come a little later it would not have been hard to work out Kingcol's destination, and the temporary bridge at Mujara would have been discovered. As it was, it remained intact, and by evening the column was trundling up

KINGCOL ROUTE 1941

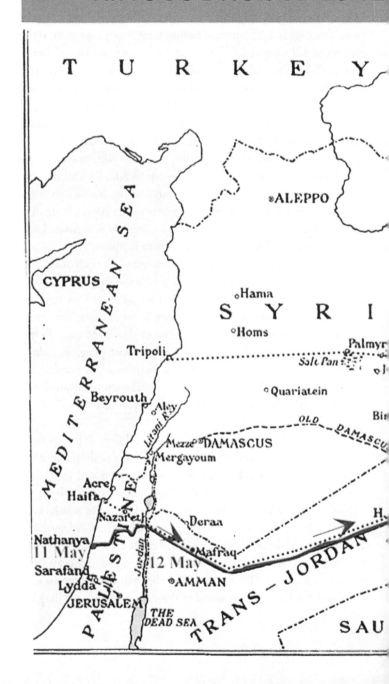

Palestine to Habbaniya

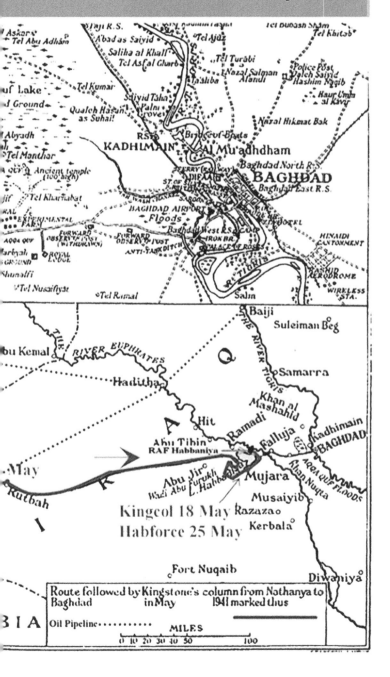

Route followed by Kingstone's column from Nathanya to Baghdad in May 1941 marked thus

Oil Pipeline·········· MILES
0 10 20 30 40 50   100

Kingcol 18 May
Habforce 25 May

the road and setting up camp around the Imperial Airways rest house beside the lake. Dunford Wood, like the rest of the camp, was relieved: *"The 'Phantom Column' has arrived,"* he wrote the next day.

Somerset de Chair described it to a war correspondent at Habbaniya at the time as *"one of the greatest marches in history... the first time since the days of Alexander the Great that an army has succeeded in crossing the desert from the shores of the Mediterranean to the banks of the Euphrates,"* an assertion that was repeated to millions around the world in a neat piece of propaganda. In fact it was not quite true, as in the 7th Century the Muslim warrior Khalid ibn al-Walid had crossed Iraq in the opposite direction in his conquest of the Arab tribes. But as de Chair remarked in The Golden Carpet, *'That is the trade secret of history - to write it yourself as you go."* Still, it was a remarkable feat.

In addition to Kingcol, other reinforcements had been steadily trickling into Habbaniya over the previous week. Following the original landings of the 20th Indian Brigade at Basra in mid April and then again on the 29th, the 21st Indian Brigade had arrived from India on 6th May, enabling the British to gain full control of the city. Since they still lacked transport for an advance north, a route which in any case was fraught with difficulty due to the extensive flooding of the Tigris and Euphrates, a decision was made to airlift more troops to Habbaniya now that the siege had been broken, and in the second week of May elements of the 2nd Battalion of the 4th Gurkha Rifles began arriving in Vincents and DC2s. To maintain momentum, Colonel Roberts was keen to press on to Fallujah and capture the strategic Iron Bridge, a key link on the road to Baghdad thirty miles to the east. With the arrival of the Luftwaffe, this was now more critical than ever. He had wanted to move earlier, but needed to wait for the artillery of Kingcol. So a plan was drawn up to start the advance on the town on the night of the 18th, with more units to follow on the 19th.

Meanwhile air reinforcements continued to arrive.[3] Following the appearance of the two long range Hurricanes on the 16th, the next day four more Gladiators and six more Blenheims flew in from Egypt, and that evening the Blenheims and Hurricanes flew two hundred miles to attack Mosul air base. They flew low level, so as to avoid being spotted by any roving German reconnaissance planes.

Despite the loss of one of the Hurricanes,[4] two of Junck's planes were destroyed on the ground and four damaged, and the next day two Gladiators from the Air Striking Force, on reconnaissance and message dropping duties over Baghdad, came across two ME110s preparing to take off from Hinaidi Air Base. They missed hitting them as they took off but shot them both down in the subsequent dogfight, which was an amazing result considering the capability mismatch. It turned out that the two German planes had no rear gunners - they had been used to transport Junck's planning officers for the conference in Baghdad, and were now returning to Mosul without them.[5]

Since Junck's arrival, within the space of two days, his force had been whittled down to just four serviceable Heinkels and eight ME100s - a loss of thirty percent of his force. Meanwhile the RAF at Habbaniya was in much better shape, and by the 18th they numbered thirteen Gladiators and five Hurricanes in 'A' Squadron, all the remaining Audaxes, Oxfords and Gordons split between 'B', 'C' and 'D' Squadrons, and fourteen Blenheims in two detachments of seven each, from 84 and 203 Squadrons. However, the British Chiefs of Staff remained worried. Throughout May the War Cabinet briefing notes were reporting a build-up of German forces and 'tourists' in Syria with the connivance of the French, along with arms shipments arriving by train in Mosul. According to one estimate, the Germans had at their disposal up to sixty aircraft to send to Iraq.

There were wider implications too. Eden told Churchill on 19th May that *"these developments cause me the most concern on account of their influence on Turkey's policy. The Turks are concentrating troops on the Iraqi and Syrian frontiers, and are asking us in return for our plans for dealing with the situation in these recalcitrant countries."* [6]

There was not a moment to lose.

~

1 The Golden Carpet, Somerset de Chair, p 54.
2 From the Arabic word for 'fifty', dry, hot sand-filled windstorms that blow sporadically a fifty-day period in Spring, hence the name. It can last for several hours, carrying great quantities of sand and dust with a speed of up to 100 MPH.
3 The Wellingtons at Shaibah had been withdrawn back to Egypt after the lifting of the siege.
4 The pilot, McRobert, was the second of three brothers to be killed in the war. According to Dudgeon, their mother later presented a Stirling bomber to the RAF with the name 'MacRobert's Reply', which she had funded to the tune of £25,000. The War That Never Was, Tony Dudgeon, p150.
5 The War That Never Was, Tony Dudgeon, p151.
6 Gulf War Command, Ashley Jackson, p222.

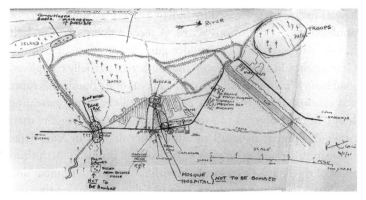

A hand drawn map detailing the Fallujah attack plan for the RAF, identifying the mosque and a prominent sheikh's house, 'NOT to be bombed', and some camouflaged boats top left to 'machine gun if possible'.

The Attack on Falluja

THE SAME DAY THAT KINGCOL ARRIVED in Habbaniya, Air Vice-Marshal D'Albiac flew in from Palestine to take over as AOC, and Major General Clark arrived from H4 to take command of the land forces. He found Colonel Roberts' planned attack on Fallujah about to begin.

The plan was an innovative one. Faced with the extensive floods, Roberts had split the troops into five columns, organised as the 'Habbaniya Brigade'. Three of the columns, including a force of Levies, the armoured cars, Habbaniya's captured 3.7 inch howitzers and the recently airlifted 2/4 Gurkhas, would cross the river via an improvised ferry at Sin el Dhibban and approach from the west, making sure to cut off the route for any reinforcements from the Iraqi Brigade holed up in Ramadi. This was no small task, as the river was 750 feet wide with a strong current, and a 1,500 metre hawser had to be fashioned by Indian Sappers[1] to hold a series of pontoons to get the troops across. A second group of a hundred Levies with Kingcol's 25-pounder guns, led by Captain Alistair Graham, would approach from the south via a partially completed road from Mujarra to Fallujah called Hammond's Bund. This route was elevated above the floods but had been cut by the retreating Iraqis, so the troops had to wade across the breach dragging their heavy equipment in small pleasure boats drafted in from Lake Habbaniya, as well as on rafts made from oil drums.[2] Last, a third force of the King's Own would be airlifted in Bristol Bombay and Valentia aircraft at dawn to the east of Fallujah to cut off the road to Baghdad.

However, the force was still a small one, and if the Iraqis made a determined stand in the city, crowded as it was with civilians, it would likely prove difficult to overcome them without significant loss of civilian life. So before the troops went in, it was hoped that a combination of bluff and terror from the air would force the Iraqis to flee or surrender, as had happened on the escarpment two weeks earlier.

The crossings took place on the night of the 18th May. The first column across the river became severely delayed, but the Levies under Graham made it over the two hundred yard gap of Hammonds Bund by dawn, in time to be in position for the bombing blitz by the Air Striking Force, which was followed later in the morning with a leaflet drop. These outlined in Arabic and in graphic detail the overwhelming British forces advancing from all sides. In addition, two Audaxes from 'C' Squadron flew over Fallujah at dawn to cut the telegraph wires - in one case by slicing through them with a wing.[3]

The attack on Fallujah was one of the first combined air and land operations under unified command in any war. Dunford Wood described the role of 'C' Squadron:

"Yesterday a proper operation order came out, for the

investment of Fallujah by Levies and the King's Own on the Plain (going there at dawn in Valentias). The RAF are then to bomb the hell out of it, the bombing being interspersed with pamphlets, until the troops there surrender. I have two salvoes, miss the cemetery and brick kiln, and nearly get taken off the show, as they all land in the desert. Then I put four through the bazaar roof, and four bounce off its walls, so I get a bullseye. 4,000 ft – 2,000 ft seemed to do the trick. But the town hasn't surrendered, and no one thought of what to do if they didn't, at least the army didn't, so the AOC has now ordered them to capture Fallujah."

Contrary to the typically dismissive comment from an RAF officer about Army organisation, in fact there was a very well formed plan, though risky with a force of only five hundred. With the Iraqi forces showing no signs of surrendering, despite the ferocious barrage, a renewed bombardment was unleashed shortly after 14:00, in which Kingcol's 25-pounders took part, supported by a dive bombing attack by the Audaxes using customised bombs that had organ fluting attached to their fins that emitted a screaming noise as they fell. Then the signal was given, and Captain Graham's Levies rushed the bridge, capturing it intact. There is some debate about whether they were opposed or not. But what is certain, is that the bulk of the Iraqi troops had disappeared.

One of the Assyrian soldiers, Khamshi Odisho Moshe, years later recalled the attack on the Iron Bridge:

"The CO (Captain Graham) told us to cross the river at night because the way was clear up to Hammonds Bund. We crossed and took up defensive positions on the left flank. We were ordered not to attack until our Bombers arrived... When the Bombers and the Guns finish their job, our attack will begin.

> *The planes arrived and started their work, the bombing was very intense. At that time my job was a rangefinder and a Vickers Gunner... Zero hour we were told was 3.45 PM, the time we would attack with 65 Assyrian Levies. The attack was very fierce, our boys wanted revenge for Semele,[4] the enemy had two choices, stay and die or run! We captured 18 Vickers machine guns in that attack. Then the whole company joined in the clearing of the town."[5]*

Those Iraqi troops who did not flee discarded their uniforms and melted away into the civilian population, though quite a few were picked up on account of their precious Iraqi army boots, which they were loathe to jettison. Three hundred men, plus a General and twenty-six officers, were found sheltering in the town hospital, and they were immediately taken prisoner. In all, the Air Striking Force had flown 134 sorties that day and dropped ten tons of bombs.

The British propaganda machine was soon in operation. The Basrah Times reported:

> *"The rebel Iraq Army fled in disorder from Fallujah yesterday when they were attacked from three sides by British and loyal Arab troops. There were no British casualties. The inhabitants of Fallujah welcomed the troops and the restoration of law and order."[6]*

In fact the city remained shuttered, and what few Arabs were on the streets were sullen and uncooperative.

The Daily Bulletin issued on May 20th by the Intelligence Branch of Air HQ at Habbaniya was equally effusive:

> *"The whole operation was a very fine example of cooperation between the Royal Air Force and the Army.*

Intelligence Branch,
Air Headquarters,
British Forces in 'Iraq,
HABBANIYA.   'IRAQ.

20.5.41.   DAILY BULLETIN.   Serial No. 16.

LOCAL NEWS.

FALLUJA was captured yesterday. The operations
started during the late evening of the previous day, when
columns of our troops moved forward under cover of darkness
to positions surrounding FALLUJA on three sides. At 05.00
hours local time, a very heavy bombing attack was launched
on the enemy troop positions in the town, and further attacks
were carried out during the course of the day until, by 14.00
hours local time, our land forces were able to rush the
bridge and establish themselves inside the town.

The whole operation was a very fine example of
co-operation between the Royal Air Force and the Army.

The results of this success are important as
FALLUJA Bridge is a most important defile between BAGHDAD and
the route to the West; and the success achieved was notable
for having cost us no casualties whatever, either Army or
Air Force. The enemy, however, suffered heavily, and in
addition to those killed in action, they left many prisoners
in our hands.

Balls! - Daily Bulletin no. 16, marked 'Off(icers) Mess'.

*The results of this success are important, as Fallujah
Bridge is the most important defile between Baghdad
and the route to the West; and the success achieved
was notable for having cost us no casualties whatever,
either Army or Air Force. The enemy, however, suffered
heavily, and in addition to those killed in action, they
left many prisoners in our hands."*

On Dunford Wood's copy of this bulletin, ten copies of which
were reserved for 4 SFTS, someone had scrawled *'Balls'*. Dudgeon
also expressed some scepticism of the Army's actions, claiming
credit for what the RAF felt was, once again, their victory.[7]

However, Major General Clark's official report on the action
ended as follows:[8]

> *To sum up the results of this battle, I think the cricket score board would have shown something like the following:*

> *Iraqi Army: Frightened out; Bowler: RAF; Score: 0*

So at least Clark acknowledged that the bowler had been the RAF. Dunford Wood also used a cricketing metaphor, but for a very different reason. Just before the advance to Fallujah he had been sent on two reconnaissance sorties:

> *"Today I do two half hour patrols and shoot up some derelict cars on the desert road out of Ramadi. I spot 17 lorries on the left bank of the Euphrates opposite the ferry pier at Ramadi, and the boys go out to bomb them. Then I see a car on Fallujah Plain. It sees me too, stops, and out get the passengers, being in too much of a hurry to shut the doors. I front gun the car, and notice the passengers are Arabs with rifles. I give one long burst, and I see one man lying in the sand and his body vanishes under the dust spurts, but he gets up afterward and runs off. I go down on another, but the Vickers jams, and whilst clearing it, I think this game is hardly cricket, so push off home and leave them."* [9]

Following his victory, Colonel Roberts relinquished command to Clark and flew back to Basrah, and the bulk of the troops were withdrawn to Habbaniya. Just several companies of Levies and a company of the King's Own were left behind to secure the town.

There was an interesting postscript to this battle. Despite its undoubted success the new AOC, Air Vice-Marshal d'Albiac, who had only arrived the day before, was unhappy with what he saw as the "mis-employment" of air power that had regrettably set "an undesirable precedent". He disliked the way the RAF had been used by the army, directly under the command of the Army commander, Roberts. In his opinion, the army should have managed alone, freeing up the aircraft to concentrate on destroying the Luftwaffe. It was an odd position to take, having just returned from Greece where the Germans had used their air force so effectively in close support of their troops, but it shows how innovative Roberts's scheme had really been. It also serves to illustrate the strong rivalry between the RAF and the Army, echoing Dudgeon and Dunford Wood's comments. The RAF joked, not without reason, that the 'phantom column' had arrived ten days too late, to find that the camp had relieved itself.

But despite their frustration, three days later the Army would finally 'earn their spurs'.

~

1. No 10 Field Company of the Madras Sappers and Miners, flown in from Basra.
2. The Levies were made to practise in small boats in Habbaniya's outdoor swimming pool in the days beforehand.
3. The 'C' Squadron operations book written up by Haig and Dunford Wood noted the method employed by the second Audax: *"Before dawn F/O Arthur, with P/O Irwin as air gunner, landed on Fallujah Plain and cut the enemy communications with Baghdad. The method employed here is perhaps worthy of note. The pilot taxied his plane under the wires, then standing on his gravity tank cut them with a pair of garden shears, while his rear gunner covered the operation with a Bren gun mounted on the plain."* C' Squadron historical record, P/O Allan Haig and P/O Dunford Wood.
4. Semele was the site of an infamous massacre of the Assyrian minority by the Iraqi Army in 1936. It was one of the reasons the Assyrian Levies remained loyal to the British.
5. As quoted in an an interview recorded at http://assyrianlevies.info
6. Gulf War Command, Ashley Jackson, p240.
7. The War That Never Was, Tony Dudgeon, p157: *"By late morning there seemed to be very little movement of any sort and by 1pm there was nothing at all for us to see from above. We told the Army so, and invited them in to capture the bridge. Politely they declined, suggesting it might be a trap, and anyway their troops were totally untrained for street fighting. This was very irritating."*
8. http://www.morvalearth.co.uk
9. The War Diaries of Colin Dunford Wood, Vol 1, 15th May 1941.

*The British Embassy under siege, May 1941,
with people sleeping on the lawn.*

Final Preparations

In the British Embassy in Baghdad, a bar was opened each day at 18:00 under the palm trees in the garden, and everyone would gather with their single rationed drink to hear Dr Sindersen's evening garrison news, which bizarrely, to keep morale up, he presented in rhyme.

Spirits were also bolstered with the continued flying of the Union Jack in the courtyard. Early on in the siege, the Iraqi foreign-affairs ministry had sent the ambassador a note demanding that the British flag over the embassy be taken down, as flying it at a time when Britain was 'waging war on Iraq' would provoke 'a regrettable incident'. To avoid provocation, Ambassador Cornwallis had acquiesced, dependent as he was on the foreign ministry for his food supplies, water and electricity, but had instead raised it on a flagpole erected in the courtyard, from where it was not visible outside.

For days there had been very little news, and no sign of any relief column. All they'd heard were bland news reports on the BBC that the situation in Iraq had 'stabilised', which was the last thing they wanted. And on the 19th, on hearing on the BBC that the Iraq situation was 'developing satisfactorily', Stark wrote *"Adrian Holman (the counsellor) can't see the satisfactorily; I say I can't even see the developing."* [1]

Nor had there been any discernible movement from the Indian Brigades which had been landed in the south a month ago, judging by the occasional reports they received of minor skirmishes around Basrah. It was 350 miles away. Dr Sinderson's rhyming report of their progress one evening was scathing:

> *"If three brigades in seven weeks,*
> *advance for half a mile,*
> *'Were it not well', the General said,*
> *'that they should rest awhile?'*
> *'I doubt it,' said the AOC,*
> *and smiled a bitter smile."* [2]

Freya Stark explained the calculations - the last time a British army had marched on Baghdad from Basrah, during the Mesopotamian campaign in the First World War, it had taken three years! Gloom descended.

However, the 20th brought the first good news for weeks, that Fallujah had been captured. That was just thirty miles away.

> *"Thank God," noted Freya Stark. "It really brings relief in sight. Hope Ramadi and tribes may follow."*

The police guarding the embassy started to become noticeably friendlier, allowing in all sorts of supplies,[3] including large quantities of cosmetics, and it was clear that Rashid Ali's coup against the British did not have wide popular support, especially now it was faltering. The policemen at the gate even made a joke of it, remarking how strange it was that *"those Englishwomen still think about cosmetics when they are going to be massacred in three days."*[4]

The day after the capture of Fallujah, the Luftwaffe made another determined attack against British forces, both in Fallujah and Habbaniya. The Hurricanes and Gladiators were kept busy most of the day. In the early morning, 'C' Squadron of Audaxes, supported by Gladiators, went off to bomb Hinaidi air base. Dunford Wood writes of losing his way and going on alone, and bemoans the fact that his bombing is not much good. Later that afternoon, he reports Heinkels bombing the hangars and a number of ME110s strafing the camp. Several Blenheims are damaged and one is destroyed, along with two Valentias and a DC2.

Two days later, unexpectedly, the Iraqis launched a surprise counter attack on Fallujah at 03:00, supported by a number of light Fiat tanks. This was almost certainly planned with the help of German advisors in Baghdad, and it followed an attack plan that had been rehearsed the year before in war games organised for the Iraqi army by British advisors.

For a while the thin screen of British defenders were under severe pressure, the King's Own suffering a fifty percent casualty rate amongst its officers. Sniping erupted from civilian rooftops, and there was bitter house to house fighting. But they held, just, supported by a counterattack from the Levies who had remained to garrison the town. Brigadier Kingstone, alerted to the situation at 04:00, went forward from Habbaniya to take charge, and later in the day a squadron of the Household Cavalry and two companies of 1 Essex waded across Hammonds Bund to bolster the defence, lugging their equipment the seven miles to Fallujah on foot.

The Air striking Force was also scrambled into action. Here's Dunford Wood's diary entry for the 22nd:

> "This morning woken up at 5am, as Fallujah is being attacked, and Haig, Figgis and self go off. I put a stick amongst some lorries and miss two cars going flat out, with two bombs apiece. Front gun jams so I have to come home, quarter of an hour after the other two, to find the camp being bombed, and 110s just finished and they all think I have "gone for a Burton", as the expression is here.[5]

> Off we go again and we spot the Iraqi troops attacking Fallujah, I find a lot in holes and a road cutting, with two lorries under desert coloured hoods. I miss them with both sticks, but reckon I got some troops. I nearly fail to pull out of the second dive. Then down with the Vickers and two long, long bursts at the troops, who sit up and fire their rifles at me. Then No. 3 stoppage (gun jam) so off home. The first sortie I got a No. 1 (stoppage) every time after about 15 seconds. A pity, as I had a runabout at my mercy, filled with troops with white hat bands crouching on the floor and hanging on the foot boards. I always cut my knuckles on these damn bomb levers, and a bad one today."[6]

Eventually the Iraqis were repulsed, but the King's Own suffered fifty casualties, the most in the entire campaign so far. If the RAF had any doubts about their bravery, they would certainly have been reassured that day.

§

The next few days were spent in planning and waiting. The road to Baghdad was clear, but the British were not yet ready to advance, preferring to wait for the remainder of Habforce who were due to arrive on the 25th. Even when they did, the entire force would still number a fraction of the 40,000 the Iraqis could field, with their brigade at Ramadi, and divisions in Baghdad and Mosul.

There was also a debate about the potency of the Luftwaffe. Despite their heavy losses, it was thought that additional planes had been getting through. However, their bombing runs were becoming more sporadic, and German documents show that by the 21st, they had just two serviceable Heinkels left, both of which were able to fly only by cannibalising parts from other planes. The wear and tear on the planes from the desert conditions was becoming unsustainable, given that there had been no time to properly 'tropicalise' them - for example they had no sand filters, and the silicone from the sand was destroying their pistons.[7]

Junck had other problems too. In addition to his forces draining away, he was losing confidence in Grobba, who was still reporting confidently back to Berlin that all was well and that the Iraqis would prevail. On the 23rd Junck asked for a conference with his superiors in Athens. The same day, Hitler finally issued a directive aimed at the Middle East problem - *Directive 23*:

> *"The Arab Freedom Movement is our natural ally against England in the Middle East. In this context the uprising in Iraq is of special importance. I have therefore decided to hasten developments in the Middle East by supporting Iraq."*

But it was too little, too late. No more practical help was offered than had already been provided. The very first paragraph showed Junck where Hitler's priorities lay:

> *"Whether and how it may be possible, in conjunction with an offensive against the Suez Canal, finally to break the British position between the Mediterranean and the Persian Gulf is a question that will be answered only after Barbarossa."*

The stable door was being firmly closed after the proverbial horse had bolted.

§

Preparations for the advance by Kingcol on Baghdad were begun on the 23rd. That morning, a force of the Arab Legion under Glubb with a Royal Engineer officer and two armoured cars were ferried across the Euphrates at Sin el Dhibban and tasked with reaching the Mosul-Baghdad railway at Samarra, seventy-five miles to the north, and blowing it up. Intelligence was received that further supplies of arms and ammunition were arriving at Mosul from Syria, so it was important to prevent them reaching the Iraqis in Baghdad.

When the British force arrived at sunset, they failed to find a bridge to destroy, so they ripped up some rails and returned to Habbaniya. But as a public relations exercise it was invaluable - Glubb's appearance in the tribal areas gave the lie to the Iraqis' claims that he had been killed at Rutbah.

The next day, another attempt was made to disrupt the railway - this time the line between Aleppo and Mosul. For this operation, a party of thirteen sappers was airlifted in a Valentia to an area close to Campaniya in north-east Syria, where they demolished a major rail viaduct with explosives. Though they were fired on by a Vichy armoured car on take off, they managed to return to Habbaniya unscathed. For the moment, any supplies from Syria to Mosul and from Mosul to Baghdad would be severely disrupted.

On the 23rd, Wavell flew from Cairo to Basrah to confer with Auckinleck, who had travelled from India, to make final plans for the capture of Baghdad and to discuss the future of Iraq. Unbeknownst to Wavell, Churchill had just a few days earlier made the decision to replace Wavell with Auckinleck, and send Wavell by return to take over as C-in-C India. Crete was going badly, the Iraq episode had been mishandled, and more recently Wavell had been pushing back on a directive from London to support the Free French in a move against Vichy held Syria. The General was also exhausted, physically and mentally, fighting as he was on so many fronts.

In the brief meeting in Basrah, it was agreed that Habforce would approach Baghdad from the west. Simultaneously, the two Indian brigades would finally start advancing north, one up the Euphrates, the other up the Tigris, while a third Brigade would be sent to Basrah from India to take over defence of the port, city and airfield. It was envisaged that this would take some weeks, if not months.

Auckinleck pressed the importance of moving on to Mosul and occupying the oilfields. Wavell did not disagree, but he insisted that the resources would have to come from India. He made plain his thoughts in a telegram to the CIGS, Dill, after he returned to Cairo:

> *"C-in-C Middle East to CIGS, 25th May, 1941, 09.02hrs. From discussion with Auchinleck it is obvious that we regard Iraq from somewhat different angles. My main task, defence of Egypt and Palestine, would be made more difficult but would not be greatly jeopardised by hostile control of Iraq, whereas hostile control of Syria would affect me much more closely and dangerously. So long as my resources are inadequate I am bound to be influenced by the closer and more threatening danger. India on the other hand regard Iraq as absolutely vital outpost of their defence since they consider that hostile Iraq would mean hostile Iran*

and Afghanistan and compromise whole defence of Indian Empire. Middle East is already fully occupied... troops in Iraq are mainly Indian, maintenance must be from India... To sum up, it seems that in view of her greater interest and greater stake in Iraq operations, India should resume control as soon as possible."

Dill, Wavell's friend, can't have been best pleased to receive this cable, and would have been aware that its tone would not have pleased Churchill. It seemed Wavell still did not understand that a hostile Iraq was a clear threat to the entire Middle East. The message was sent just two days before the advance towards Baghdad, and at that point both Wavell and Auckinleck had every expectation that it would be a long drawn-out campaign that would undoubtedly need more resources. In Wavell and Auckinleck's view, the main thrust was to be from Basrah - the columns due to set off from Habbaniya were viewed as diversionary, holding down Iraqi troops while the Indian Brigades came up from the south.

Those who had been doing the bulk of the fighting so far, the commanders in Habbaniya - in particular the RAF - viewed it rather differently. They had already seen how the Iraqis had no stomach for the fight. Even with a force of just 1,500, vastly outnumbered by the Iraqis, they still felt they were in with a shout. It was in that spirit that they met on the eve of their advance, on the 25th, at a commanders' conference in Air House at Habbaniya to put the finishing touches to their plan. Air Vice-Marshal D'Albiac and Major General Clark were joined by Habforce's commanders, alongside Savile and Dudgeon of the Air Striking Force. The plan was for the advance to be two-headed. One column of seven hundred men under Lieutenant Colonel Andrew Ferguson of the Household Cavalry would cross the Euphrates and advance towards Baghdad in a large loop around the floods to the north, approaching down the Mosul road. This force would include the bulk of the Household Cavalry, minus 'C' Squadron, a section of the 2nd Armoured Car Company, the Arab Legion, and a field troop of the Royal Artillery. A second column of 750 men led by Brigadier Kingstone would be made up of the remainder of the 2nd Armoured Car Company under Casano, 'C' Squadron of the Household Cavalry, two companies of 1 Essex, and the remainder of the Royal Artillery battery. Their route would take them across the floods at Hammonds Bund, this time on iron barges that had been floated up from Habbaniya to take the weight of their transport; across the Euphrates at the Iron Bridge in Fallujah; and finally over the Fallujah Plan to Khan Nuqta and the Abu Ghuraib canal, on the outskirts of Baghdad - a distance of thirty miles.

Air support would be organised into three components. A force of bombers would be kept on standby to be deployed against Iraqi troops as needed by the Army, and supplied with the new screaming bombs that the workshops had engineered, while two flights of three aircraft - a mix of Gladiators and Audaxes - would be kept on standby for reconnaissance, close support, and fighter protection.

The final question to be ironed out was how the Army would communicate where they needed support by the RAF to be deployed, given that maps were not entirely reliable, and large areas were under flood. At the end of April, Dudgeon had undertaken an aerial reconnaissance of the areas between Fallujah and Baghdad, and had made a series of maps that had been used extensively when planning aerial operations in the subsequent battle.[8] He now proposed rerunning the exercise the next day to recce Iraqi military positions and the state of the floods, and gridding the resulting photographs into squares, twenty-five per square mile. He could then re-photograph the gridded original and print them into books, to be distributed to all units.[9]

The next day he took an Oxford out at 10,000 feet, up and down the road from Fallujah to Baghdad, and by the morning of the 27th, the photo books were ready.

~

1. Dust in the Lion's Paw, Freya Stark, p105.
2. East is West, Freya Stark.
3. These were secured after the first week of the siege via an understanding with the Iraqi Ministry of Foreign Affairs, who remained cooperative throughout.
4. East is West, Freya Stark, p153/157: Stark records an amusing piece of banter the day after Fallujah had been taken, and when reports started circulating of many German planes being shot down: "The Germans are of the family of Satan," said a policeman guarding the river entrance. "I have heard,' said I, "that we have brought six of them down between Habbaniya and Syria." "Praise be to God," said the enemy, under cover of darkness. "But we have burnt forty of yours," they added as an afterthought. "I take refuge with God from your untruthfulness," said I, to which they agreed with laughter.
5. The RAF expression 'Gone for a Burton' - meaning killed or crashed - was first used in 1941 and possibly came from a pre-war advertisement for Burton beer; if someone was missing from a group, they had gone 'for a Burton'.
6. The War Diaries of Colin Dunford Wood, Vol 1, 22nd May 1941.
7. This was highlighted first hand to the Air Striking Force when they discovered an ME110 force landed and abandoned in the desert. They had it towed back to Habbaniya, where it was made serviceable, and it eventually wound up in a flying training school in Rhodesia for practising dogfights with.
8. In 'Hidden Victory' Dudgeon remembers how nervous he was during this photographic recce flight at a time when hostilities threatened to break out at any moment. He wrote that it felt like 'walking down Piccadilly with no trousers on'.
9. This was a stroke of genius, and an early example of grid references being used to locate targets on maps - a practise that became more common as the war went on and which would develop into an international grid reference system in the late 1940s.

Troops carrying a boat across Hammonds Bund.

End Game

THE FIRST TROOPS, GUNS AND TRUCKS of Kingstone's southern column had started being ferried across Hammonds Bund on the 25th, to gather in Fallujah ready for the advance on the 27th. Once again, de Chair had been detailed to help organise the logistics. The iron barges were pulled across the seventy-five yard gap - considerably narrowed in the past week in a failed attempt to fill it in entirely - on another thick steel hawser, a similar method to the one rigged up to cross the Euphrates at Sin el Dhibban. The plan was to get the column across in one night, but when the first 25-pounders started to load at dusk, it soon became apparent that it would take a lot longer, as the guns had to go separately from their tractors, and the estimation of ten minutes per vehicle turned into one hour for each of these guns. Once across the gap, they were guided along the embankment and across the seven mile stretch of desert to Fallujah, where a collection area had been organised on the edge of the town.

At daybreak, not even half the column was across, and since the crossing was vulnerable to air attack, the remaining vehicles had to disperse into the desert while the ferry was dismantled until the following night.

The northern column, meanwhile, left on the afternoon of 27th, crossing the Euphrates via the Sin el Dhibban hawser ferry. Led by the Arab Legion, they raced across the desert to the north of Fallujah without meeting any opposition, and late at night arrived near Taji, just six miles to the north of Baghdad. Undetected, they bivouacked for the night.

In the end it took three nights to get the entire southern column across, and the start of the advance had to be postponed until the 28th. Fortunately there were no more attacks on the column from the Luftwaffe, who were evidently down to their last planes. However, there were a number of desultory attacks on the camp. On the 25th Dunford Wood reported:

> *"Two doses of ME110s yesterday and the first finds us all in the tent and we all get hurt jumping into the same trench. Today a lackadaisical blitz on Ramadi, but I don't go up and haven't done so for two days now. Then some bombing by a lone Heinkel, and three 110s sweep by over the polo pitch and away."* [1]

And on the 27th:

> *"I go and bomb empty palm groves at Ramadi on the evening of the 25th and go off for a second trip. Then up again to bomb the military school at Mushaid point, but bloody awful. Heinkels at 0650 yesterday, but today's dose not yet delivered. Blenheims continually firing up Mosul. Met Masters* [2] *of 2/4 GR in the*

198

Club last night, shooting a line about battles around Basrah. A lot of funny fellows arrive in Blenheims here and recount their experiences in Greece innumerable times." [3]

The attacks on Ramadi he referred to were carried out by the Air Striking Force to keep the Iraqi Brigade tied up there while Habforce advanced west. A squadron of the Household Cavalry was also kept back with armoured cars of the 1st Armoured Car Company to cover the Ramadi - Habbaniya road, to prevent the Iraqis escaping, and between the 24th and 26th it was in action against the same force that had met Glubb's force at Rutbah, under Fawzi el-Qawujki. They were forced to abandon two armoured cars, and eventually retreat to Habbaniya. It was clear there were considerable scattered units of Iraqis in the vicinity of Ramadi and Fallujah, still full of fight, but luckily for the British, not coordinated.

Just after 04:00 the southern column finally left Fallujah. The first contact with the enemy was the police post at Khan Nuqta an hour later, but in the event the small Iraqi force there surrendered, and it appeared that an Iraqi battalion had only just withdrawn. Where to, no one could tell, but it was clear that the command post had only recently been vacated, evidenced by an uneaten breakfast. On interrogation, it was discovered that a series of trenches had been dug in the road ahead, and then submerged by opening up the sluice gates of the Abu Ghuraib canal regulator, ready to catch the unwary. So engineers were sent ahead with the armoured cars with steel ramps, to bridge the gaps.

It was at this point that the third and final deciding factor in the battle occurred, and it turned out to be a true stroke of genius. At the Iraqi command post, alongside the uneaten breakfast, De Chair stumbled on a telephone switchboard with an open line. He and his interpreter cranked the handle to see what they could find. De Chair recounted what happened next:

"Reading (his Palestinian interpreter) almost dropped the receiver in his excitement as an agitated voice at the other end called in Iraqi: 'Nam-Nam. I've been trying to raise you for two hours. What is the matter?' I said, 'Tell them that we are surrounded by the British; that the British have got tanks, and that the tanks are already across the floods.'

Reading spoke to the distant operator in an admirably excited voice, laying horrified stress on the word 'Bababa' - tanks. Consternation followed at the other end, the operator evidently rushing away with his news. I thought it inadvisable to try any more deception, as the enemy might grow suspicious, but I kept Reading on the line, never dreaming what a rich harvest we were going to reap.... They babbled on in greater and greater alarm. A patrol was ordered out by the headquarters of the (Iraqi) 3rd Division to report on the presence of British tanks and reported in a great state of agitation later in the morning (we could scarcely believe it) that the British had at least 50 tanks, of which 15 were already across the floods. A despairing artillery commander, who was indeed shelling us wildly, cried out over the telephone that he was 'engaging a formation of five British tanks' (which could only be Casano's three armoured cars with their high conning towers, and two tenders)..." [4]

It was both an amazing deception, and an incredible stroke of luck. The ramifications can hardly be underestimated, as the Iraqis retreated in disarray before the flimsy British force. That afternoon Grobba sent a panicked message back to Berlin that the British were advancing on Baghdad with a hundred tanks. By that point, the Luftwaffe had no serviceable ME110s left, and just two Heinkels with four bombs. In twenty-four hours, Rashid Ali would be gone.

That night, the column bedded down just before the Abu Ghuraib canal, twelve miles from Baghdad, having driven along the flooded road with the help of the Royal Engineers who laid steel ramps over where the Iraqis had dug ditches. It was as far as they could go, because the bridge over the canal had been destroyed by the Iraqis.

The next day was spent waiting while the Royal Engineers erected a temporary bridge over the canal. Meanwhile the northern Column, having captured the railway station at Taji, attempted a move south towards Baghdad but met stiff resistance. Ironically, if they had continued their advance the previous evening, they could have driven into the centre of the city, because the Iraqis were taken completely by surprise.

It was at this late juncture that a new threat emerged. While waiting for the engineers to build them a crossing, Kingstone called up air support to bomb the Iraqi forces on the other side of the canal, as shelling was coming across. Dunford Wood was in the Audax flight that was on standby, and they took off in the morning with a Gladiator to cover them.

> *"Yesterday 'Kingcol' advanced on Baghdad. A canal had been dug across the road at Khan Nuqta, and the road flooded further down beyond that. We stand by all day to support them, but only one flight required, to attack some 1,500-3,000 tribesmen massing south of Fallujah Plain. These turned out to be sheep. Today Arthur, White and self go off to attack enemy 'targets' in front of our advance guard, some 10-12 miles down the road from Khan Nuqta. We have as escort one Gladiator, W/C Wrightman, and before we arrive he is attacked by three CR42s. We break formation and go down on the deck and see him shoot one down, the*

201

pilot sort of stepping out in his parachute like going down a lift. We fly low over him and his burnt out plane and he looks Italian in long trousers and a shirt, holding up his hands in surrender. We had previously seen what we thought were Audaxes ground strafing, but which were really CR42s pulling out after diving on Wrightman.

I attack some lorries and miss each time and White puts them on fire. I machine gun one and then see our troops creeping forward and mortar smoke and explosions on the edge of a wood so go down to look for a target in it. Am below 1,000 ft when a burst comes up by my left elbow. It is deflected by a Lewis gun drum, but wounds my gunner, Williams, in the back. Only a deep graze I think but I push off home, to find the whole squadron waiting anxiously on the polo ground as we are a long time away, and CR42s had been reported there during our absence." [5]

The Fiat CR42s were from an Italian squadron[6] that had just arrived in Kirkuk via Rhodes. Belatedly, Mussolini had ordered his forces to support the Iraqis, but further delay had been caused by the Vichy French initially refusing them refuelling rights in Aleppo, spooked as they were by the RAF raids. They finally arrived just as the Luftwaffe was preparing to withdraw. De Chair witnessed the action from the ground:

"We were all busy watching the spectacle when one of the enemy aircraft began to fall in flames, the dark smoke trailing upwards, and suddenly a brilliant white parachute opened up against the blue of the sky and began to drop. I...began running in the direction of the falling airman." [7]

202

The plane had crashed on the other side of the Abu Ghuraib canal, so de Chair was forced to swim across to capture the airman. When he got to him, the only word he was heard to utter was 'stanco' - nor surprising, de Chair noted, as it transpired that the Italian had flown in from Rhodes only the day before and gone straight into action.

By the following morning, the 30th, the bridge over the canal was complete and the column moved slowly across. The shelling became more intense as they inched their way across a patchwork of irrigation canals, while the armoured cars skirmished with Iraqi troops ahead. The domes and minarets of Baghdad were now clearly visible across the fields, and the royal residence, the Palace of Roses, was just a mile from where they set up their forward observation post. Sporadic fighting continued all day, but their rapid advance had slowed to a crawl, and had finally come to a halt at a wide anti-tank ditch of the edge of the Washash canal, marking the boundary of Baghdad, from the other side of which Iraqi machine guns spewed sporadic fire.

Across the canal was the Washash army barracks. 'C' Squadron of the Air Striking Force was called up in the afternoon to bomb it with their new screaming bombs. This time Dunford Wood's bombing was more accurate:

> "Went and bombed Washash Camp, across the Iron Bridge and near the King's Palace at Baghdad. I put a stick between the ends of two long barracks, hitting both, then four 20 lb bombs through the roof of another one."[8]

The northern column, too, found the going tough to the north of Baghdad, and were pinned down just a few miles outside the city perimeter at Khadimain. It was the site of one of Iraq's revered mosques, and was fiercely defended. With the Tigris to the east and impassable marshes to the west, it was a natural line of defence for the Iraqis. One Household Cavalry trooper was killed and five injured by heavy machine gun fire, and Ferguson's men were forced to retreat. However, they had cut both rail and telephone communications with Mosul, which added to the Iraqis' impression that Baghdad was surrounded.

Then, that evening, things started to move quickly. Earlier in the day de Chair had heard from a local tribal chief, who had come to pay his respects to 'the victorious English', that Rashid Ali had fled. Rumours too had reached Habbaniya. Suddenly a fleet of cars arrived up the road from Habbaniya, together with a group of war correspondents. In the cars were Iraqi dignitaries from the government in exile of the deposed Regent, who had arrived back in Habbaniya from Syria a few days previously. With them was a British Foreign Office official, Gerald de Gaury.

The Iraqi barrage was still continuing furiously. De Chair describes the final act of this extraordinary campaign:

> *"I may have dozed half an hour, not more, for it was only a quarter past midnight by the luminous dial of my wrist-watch when I heard (the C/O) waking up the Brigadier.*
>
> *'An odd sort of message has come in,' the C/O was saying. 'Two delegates from the Iraqi army will appear on the Iron Bridge at two o'clock in the morning. Will we send two officers to meet them to discuss terms of armistice.'"* [9]

De Chair was detailed with another officer to go forward to the anti-tank ditch to meet the Iraqi representatives, but no one appeared. A new message arrived, to say the rendezvous had been pushed back to 04:00. Shortly before the allotted time, another car arrived from Habbaniya, this time with the AOC, d'Albiac, and Major General Clark as passengers, with Glubb. Shortly afterwards, a car appeared from the Iraqi side with flashing headlights, and there was, according to de Chair, an unseemly rush between the two commanders to be the first to meet the Iraqis.

It was agreed that one of the Iraqis was to be kept behind as a hostage, while the second was to take de Gaury along with de Chair and another officer to the British Embassy to see Ambassador Cornwallis with a message from Clark. But Clark hadn't brought anything to write on or with, so de Chair was sent off to find something. He returned with a message pad and a pencil:

> "*To HM Ambassador, British Embassy, Baghdad. A.O.C. and self have met the delegates. I have ordered advance to stand fast as from 04:00 hours. I have here in my possession the instructions of my C-in-C, General Wavell, regarding terms. A.O.C. and I will be grateful if you could see your way to come out here for discussion. We will await your instructions.*" [10]

The three British representatives were then blindfolded for the drive across the bridge into Baghdad to the British Embassy. There they found Cornwallis in bed '*with a blue cummerbund round his middle. He sat up in bed like one accustomed to focussing his mind on important and unexpected affairs at all hours of the night.*'

It transpired that earlier that day the Mayor of Baghdad, together with an Iraqi Army colonel, had visited the Ambassador and told him that Rashid Ali, on hearing the intelligence about the number of British tanks and troops surrounding the city, had fled to Iran the previous night, along with a party of forty followers, including the Red Fox and the Colonels of the 'Golden Square'. The Mayor explained that he was now in charge, and he requested an armistice. He brought with him the embassy's confiscated radio transmitter, so that Cornwallis could reestablish communication with Middle East headquarters in Cairo. Cornwallis promptly did, relaying the news to Wavell, but it took until midnight to get a message back to Habbaniya and then through a sandstorm to Brigadier Kingstone on the front line.

According to Freya Stark's account, the Iraqis begged that their constitution not be taken away.

> *"H.E. has made a wonderful speech in Arabic telling them that as he and King Feisal made the constitution, it is safe in his hands." The Mayor is "smiling three times round his face: the young officers are also very friendly - a feeling of family reunion and bygones be bygones..."* [11]

While the ambassador dressed, de Chair and his companions were feted throughout the embassy:

> *"Men and women were sleeping everywhere - on the lawns, under the porch... People crowded eagerly around us, scarcely able to believe their eyes. And so their ordeal was ended..."* [12]

Cornwallis returned with de Chair and the others, and they spent an hour agreeing terms with d'Albiac and Clark, which Cornwallis then took back to the Mayor. Grobba had also fled, to Mosul, where he was surprised to find that Junck and his unit had flown back to Aleppo without him. *Fliegerfuhrer Irak* had lost twenty-one aircraft, ninety-five percent of the force it had started with. Ironically, just as Junck and his men arrived back in Aleppo, General Felmy flew to Syria with instructions from Hitler to boost support for Iraq. It was too late. By June 3rd, they had all gone back to Greece. Meanwhile the Italians, so recently arrived, were retracing their steps to Rhodes.

The terms were uncontentious, and later that day they were accepted by both sides. What d'Albiac termed the 'Thirty Days War' was ended.

It had been the most extraordinary campaign. Habbaniya's Air Striking Force had flown 1,600 sorties and dropped over a hundred tons of bombs, while in the final advance less than 1,500 men had forced the surrender of an army of over 20,000. As Major General Clark pointed out to de Chair, the whole success of the advance on Baghdad had hung on two threads - the two wire hawsers that took the northern column and the south column across the flooded waters of the Euphrates.

For others, it had rested on something else. Freya Stark wrote: *"We have done this with only two battalions - colossal bluff."* [13]

When one of the Iraqi armistice representatives was asked afterwards why the Iraqis had given way, his answer was simple. *"What else could we do? You have a hundred tanks there and we only had two old anti-tank guns on that front."*

But in the end, none of this would have been possible without the heroism of those thirty-nine pupil pilots and their instructors in those first few days at Habbaniya.

~

1. The War Diaries of Colin Dunford Wood, Vol 1, 25th May 1941.
2. John Masters, who wrote of his experiences in this campaign in The Road to Mandalay.
3. The War Diaries of Colin Dunford Wood, Vol 1, 27th May 1941.
4. The Golden Carpet, Somerset de Chair.
5. The War Diaries of Colin Dunford Wood, Vol 1, 29th May 1941.
6 11 CR42s arrived from 155 Squadriglia.
7. The Golden Carpet, Somerset de Chair.
8. The War Diaries of Colin Dunford Wood, Vol 1, 31st May 1941.
9. The Golden Carpet, Somerset de Chair, p 96.
10. The Golden Carpet, Somerset de Chair, p102.
11. Dust in the Lion's Paw, Freya Stark, p111.
12. The Golden Carpet, Somerset de Chair, p 104.
13. Dust in the Lion's Paw, Freya Stark, p113.

Postscript

THE ARMISTICE TERMS WERE UNUSUALLY LENIENT. The Iraqis were allowed to keep their arms and equipment and return to barracks, and the British forces were to be kept out of the city until the Regent had been given time to re-enter Baghdad and reestablish his government.

It was clear why these terms were offered, and the rationale behind them serves to explain why the entire Anglo-Iraq war and battle of Habbaniya was made so little of in the official record of World War Two. Britain was keen, first and foremost, to do nothing to undermine the Regent's legitimacy amongst the Iraqis. The last thing they wanted was to give the impression that he was being reinstated by British force of arms.

However, within Habforce, the terms were not popular. For the most part they were forced to give up the brand new British supplied equipment they had captured from the Iraqis, who were so much better equipped than they were. Vickers machine guns, Bren carriers, rifles - reluctantly they relinquished them and reverted to their ancient Hotchkiss and Lewis guns, though 1 Essex did manage to hang on to an Iraqi Bren carrier which accompanied them to the next campaign in Syria.

Second, the Foreign Office was keen to give the impression that this had been a war against an illegitimate Rashid Ali and not against Iraq or the Iraqi people, not least because relations across the whole Arab world were key to the successful maintenance of British control across the Middle East. So any humiliation - either of the Regent or the Iraqi army - would not have played well in Iraq, nor across the wider Arab world.

There was also a very practical reason why the British wanted their forces to remain outside the city until the situation was back under political control: they did not want the Iraqis to see how weak they were. Far from having one hundred tanks, they had six armoured cars in the two columns, just 1,450 men, and half a dozen 25-pounders. When the ambassador, Cornwallis, made a speech of thanks to the British relieving column, he was able to speak to them all at the head of a three sided square, without having to raise his voice. Would the armistice hold in the face of this reality? The day it was signed, Brigadier Kingstone drove into Baghdad to find fresh supplies for his troops. However, his instructions were that orders for food should be split up and distributed amongst a number of suppliers - mostly Baghdad's hotels - so that no one would be able to estimate what numbers he was seeking to feed. They would have been astounded.

As it was, despite British propaganda to the contrary, the public mood in Baghdad was one of hostility. Both Freya Stark and Somerset de Chair reported sullen looks, spitting and an air of menace. If the British army had revealed their true strength in the days immediately after the armistice was signed, trouble may well have flared up again, because although Rashid Ali and his supporters had fled, there was a dangerous split within the Iraqi Army, and it was only with the support of the battalions guarding Baghdad that the Mayor had been able to face down the rebel commanders, who still had considerable support in the ranks.

The wait outside the gates, however, was to have tragic consequences. Unable to prevail over the British, fired up elements within Baghdad vented their fury on the Jews of the city, raping, looting and murdering in an orgy of destruction that went on for thirty-six hours. This was the Farhud, or pogrom, during which over eight hundred Jews were massacred, an inevitable consequence of the pro-Palestinian and anti-Jewish propaganda that had spewed

210

out over the airwaves ever since Grobba had arrived on the scene in 1932. Amongst the worst offenders were the Baghdad police. Despite urgent pleas from the British Embassy for Kingcol to restore order, they did not budge, and it was left to the Mayor to order the Iraqi army out onto the streets on the second night of looting, when a curfew was set for 20:00 and looters shot on sight. At least seventy were killed. But it left a very bad legacy, bringing to an end more than two millennia of peaceful existence for the city's Jewish minority that dated from the time of Babylon.

So for all these reasons, the victory of the British against the Iraqis and the manner in which it was achieved was downplayed. The official reports of the time, from Clark and Smart (written on his behalf by Wing Commander Casey, who had taken charge of the Air Striking Force until d'Albiac arrived), were effusive in praise of the RAF pilots, the Levies, and the Armoured Cars. But it was in no one's interest to reveal how close they had come to losing a strategic lynchpin of their empire, not least because of the manner in which they won. This had not been the victory of a smaller but technologically superior force over a much larger one. The Iraqi Air Force had more modern planes and the Iraqi Army had more modern equipment than their opponents did. As Dunford Wood later remarked, the British had been caught 'with their pants down', and had come within a hair's breadth of losing their Middle East oil supplies and their air route to India. Disaster would have resulted if Iraq had fallen and the Germans had been allowed a toehold. Egypt and Palestine would have been outflanked, and the Axis powers would have had control of the oil that powered Egypt and the Indian empire. Could Britain then have fought on? It's debatable. The fact that they had to be rescued by a Flying Training School of instructors and barely trained pupil pilots in obsolete biplanes did not reflect well on the Foreign Office or the Commanders in Chief. Especially Wavell, whose recalcitrance nearly cost Britain dear. It certainly cost him his job.

Later, to give him his due, he admitted his error in his memoirs:

211

> *"I was inclined to accept the Turkish offer of mediation. But Winston quite rightly refused to have anything to do with it and said we must deal with the matter by our own military force...I told Winston that I was doubtful whether the force ordered across to Habbaniya was strong enough to effect its purpose, and it would leave me without any reserve whatsoever for any eventuality in Syria. He ordered me to send it, a bold and correct decision, which I always felt I should have taken myself."*

Churchill himself was in no doubt of its significance, though he laid as much stress on German failure as British success:

> *"The spirited defence of Habbaniya by the Training School was a prime factor in our success. The Germans had at their disposal an airborne force which would have given them Syria, Iraq and Persia, with their precious oil fields. Hitler certainly cast away the opportunity of taking a great prize for little cost in the Middle East. We in Britain, though pressed to the extreme, managed with scant forces to save ourselves from far-reaching and lasting injury."* [1]

Still, when Wavell came to write his dispatch in October 1942 (which was to form the basis of the official war history), he downplayed the RAF's contribution. Just four paragraphs out of fifty-nine were devoted to the Battle of Habbaniya.[2] Could it be because the flying school was leaderless for much of the time? The first paragraph notes:

> *"Hostilities broke out on 2nd May and the RAF Station was shelled intermittently until 5th May."*

There was no mention of the RAF's preemptive strike, or anything about 4 SFTS, and more space was devoted to the successful evacuation by the RAF of women and children than to its offensive actions. The last paragraph on Habbaniya concludes:

"On 6th May, however, our forces at Habbaniya succeeded in clearing the Plateau which overlooked the Cantonment at short range and in doing so captured 26 Iraqi officers and 408 other ranks, together with a considerable amount of equipment."

This gave the impression it was the ground troops that cleared the Iraqis, and the RAF story was minimised. Was it unintentional, given that Wavell was an army commander, he was far away from the action, and the whole episode was an embarrassment and one that he had not wanted to be involved in? The bulk of the despatch deals with the troops from India, the subsequent march on Baghdad, and the advance into Syria that followed the campaign.

When the report was to be published in 1946, it was sent to the Air Ministry by the War Office for comments just one day before it was due to go to the printer. It had a covering letter attached:

"This dispatch was today submitted to HM Stationery Office for publication on 14th August. It has to be at the printers by 1600 hrs 2 Aug. ("Today!" an RAF officer who received it for review has scribbled in the margin). *This dispatch had never been submitted to you previously unfortunately."*

A note from a Group Captain Brockman addressed to the Air Historical Department suggests some frustration at the late submission:

"The War Office have thrown a quick one at us – would you please have this dispatch examined as soon as possible and let me know whether there are any points you feel we ought to raise?"

Unfortunately the records department was in the middle of a move, so the RAF documents covering the period were unavailable, but a reply did come back from the Air Historical Department to the Air Ministry, on the 12th August, suggesting that the paragraph dealing with the Iraqi withdrawal should be rewritten to reflect the fact that it was the relentless RAF bombing that turned the tide, as well as RAF activity to break supply lines and ammunition coming from Baghdad, and only secondarily the night time sorties by the King's Own, (who elsewhere were reported as under-performing), and particularly the Levies. It went on:

"Wavell makes it sound as though our ground forces cleared the Iraqis off the Plateau. I think he might have mentioned the fact that our aircraft at Habbaniya were mostly trainers, etc, manned by impromptu crews, and that they did a remarkable job of work."

The final letter dated 16 August is from the War Office:

"It is regretted that the amendment requested in your letter dated 13th August 1946 was received too late for inclusion in this dispatch."

So is history recorded....

§

Finally, no campaign medals were awarded to 4 SFTS for what was subsequently dubbed the Anglo-Iraq War, but which at the time was referred to as Rashid Ali's rebellion. There were a number of bravery awards and campaign medals and clasps for army and air force personnel. Kingstone got a bar on his D.S.O. and the Armoured Cars commander Casano was awarded the Military Cross, but there was no recognition for the 4 SFTS training school pilots or crews, despite their high casualty rate. Of the nineteen pilots Dudgeon started with in his Oxford and Gordon squadron, just nine were still flying at the end of the month, the rest either dead, seriously wounded, or taken off flying duties due to mental strain. Of Dunford Wood's 'C' Squadron of Audax pilots under Ling, only five out of twelve survived unscathed to the end of May, and two of the four Musketeers were killed. Most of the dead are buried, overgrown and neglected, in Habbaniya's war cemetery.

For many years afterwards, Tony Dudgeon, who reached the rank of Air Vice-Marshal, fought to get recognition for 4 SFTS. As early as 1942, after El Alamein, he was quizzing Air Marshal Tedder in Cairo as to why the Battle of Habbaniya had got so little publicity, and how important the Air Marshal thought it had been.

> *"Well... it is a Royal Air Force epic. If the School had been overcome, the Germans would have got a foothold in Iraq. If they had then created a bridgehead behind us, through Vichy controlled Syria from Greece, our Middle East base could have been nipped out with German forces both to its east and west. We might then well have lost this war."* [3]

According to his son Mike Dudgeon, also an RAF officer, his mission became quite an obsession. The answer he got back in later years from the RAF was typically British: because 4 SFTS was a training school and not an operational unit, their pilots and crews did not qualify for a campaign medal - operation or no operation.

As if to give the lie to this Kafka-esque answer, there was one bravery award. A rear gunner called Aircraftman 1st Class Kenneth

Clifton was awarded the Distinguished Flying Medal for an act of heroism that was written up in Habbaniya's *Daily Bulletin No. 20* on the 24th May 1941:

> "A rear gunner, who had never flown before going solo, took control of one of our aircraft after the pilot had been killed, and made a good landing at Habbaniya. The aircraft was engaged in a reconnaissance flight over Ramadi. The pilot had just turned on his homeward journey when he was killed by a rifle shot. The observer, sitting beside the pilot, steadied the aircraft, and shouted to the rear gunner for help. Although he did not hear the call, the rear gunner realised that something was wrong and went forward to investigate. Telling his story later he said:
>
> 'While the observer was straightening out the aircraft, I removed the body of the pilot. I asked the observer if he could land the aircraft, and he replied that he was not too confident. I said that if he could not manage it, I would take her over and do my best to get her down, to which the observer replied 'Alright, she's yours'. I had to make two attempts to get her safely down to the aerodrome, but I managed on the second try.'"

Ironically there was some debate about whether he should be court martialed afterwards, because the observer he took over the controls from was a trainee pupil pilot who was qualified to land the plane, whereas Clifton was not, and he had put both them and the plane in danger. The medal citation in the London Gazette upgraded his achievement to 'a safe landing at the third attempt' and Dudgeon remembers the plane careering crazily towards a hangar on landing, narrowly avoiding a much larger pile-up. But in the end sense prevailed, and he was recommended for an award

- which led to much confusion in later years as being the only member of the RAF without wings above his flying medal. The bulletin continued:

> *"Asked if he had any misgivings at finding himself in sole charge of the aircraft, the gunner, who comes from Cardiff, replied 'No, as soon as I took control, I felt confident I could bring her home. Anyone would have done the same in similar circumstances.'"*

Indeed, the same could be said of the entire flying school in those frantic days in May. They brought it home.

~

1. The Second World War Volume 111, Winston Churchill, p236.
2. The National Archives AIR 2/7067 - General Sir A.P. Wavell's dispatch on operations in Iraq, 10 April 1941-12 Jan 1942. Submitted 18th October 1942 to the Secretary of State for War. Published in the London Gazette 14 August 1946. See the full text referenced in the Sources section.
3. The War That Never Was, Tony Dudgeon, p 180.

Sources

- The War Diaries of Colin Dunford Wood, Volume 1.
- www.storyofwar.com.
- The War that Never Was, by AV-M Tony Dudgeon.
- Hidden Victory, by AV-M Tony Dudgeon.
- The Golden Carpet, by Somerset de Chair.
- East is West, by Freya Stark.
- Dust in the Lion's Paw, by Freya Stark.
- Iraq 1941, by Robert Lyman.
- Dust Clouds in the Middle East, by Christopher Shores.
- In Every Place, The RAF Armoured Cars in the Middle East, 1921-53, by Nigel Warwick.
- Germany, Great Britain and the Rashid Ali al-Kilani Revolt of Spring 1941, by James Scott.
- The Passion of Max von Oppenheim, by Lionel Gossman.
- The Jinnee and the Magic Bottle - Fritz Grobba and the German Middle East Policy, by Wolfgang Schwanitz.
- Going Solo, by Roald Dahl.
- A Line in the Sand, by James Barr.
- The Road Past Mandalay, by John Masters.
- The Story of the Arab Legion, by John Bagot Glubb.
- Iraq between the Two World Wars, by Reeva Spector Simon.
- Wavell, Soldier and Statesman, by Victoria Schofield.
- The Crucible of War - Wavell's Command, by Barrie Pitt.
- Wavell, Scholar and Soldier, by John Connell.
- The Chief, by Ronald Lewin.
- Five Ventures, by Christopher Buckley.
- Of Generals and Gardens, by Peter Coates.
- Persian Gulf Command, by Ashley Jackson.
- A Reminiscence of War 1939-1945, by James Glass.
- Memoirs of a Diplomat's Wife, by Betty Holman.
- Hitler's Gulf War, by Barrie James.
- The National Archives - Cabinet papers, Air Ministry documents, War Office and Foreign Office papers.
- RAF Habbaniya Intelligence Reports (private collection).
- General Wavell's Despatch: Operations in Iraq, 1941-1942, London Gazette, August 1946.

Images and Maps

1. Map of Syria and Iraq 1941 – image of a map in and copyright CDW private collection.
2. 'The Four Musketeers' – image from and copyright CDW private collection.
3. Lieutenant-General Sir Archibald Wavell, 1938 - National Army Museum, 105396.
4. The sign at the entrance to RAF Habbaniya – courtesy of and copyright RAF Habbaniya Association.
5. An aerial view of RAF Habbaniya - image from and copyright CDW private collection.
6. Sykes-Picot map - from the collections of The National Archives (UK), catalogued under document record MPK1/426.
7. Rashid Ali, photographer unknown, public domain.
8. 1941 map of Baghdad – image of a map in and copyright CDW private collection.
9. 'HMAC' Euphrates, courtesy of and copyright John Rolph via RAF Habbaniya Association.
10. A Hart trainer taking part in the 'Demonstration Flight' – image from and copyright CDW private collection.
11. Squadron Leader A.G. 'Tony' Dudgeon, courtesy of and copyright Mike Dudgeon.
12. Operational map showing the disposition of Iraqi forces besieging Habbaniya – courtesy of and copyright Mike Dudgeon.
13. Tents on the Polo ground - image from and copyright CDW private collection.
14. Photo-reconnaissance image of Hinaidi air base – image from and copyright CDW private collection.
15. Habbaniya's aircraft hangars under attack – photographer unknown.
16. The remains of the Iraqi relief column – image from and copyright CDW private collection.
17. Churchill's message - Daily Bulletin No. 4 – image of a document in and copyright CDW private collection.
18. An armoured car of Glubb's Arab Legion – photographer unknown.
19. ME110s of Fliegerfuhrer Irak being prepared in the Balkans – photographer unknown, public domain.

20. Elements of Kingcol in the desert, courtesy of and copyright Dr C D E Morris via RAF Habbaniya Association.

21. Map of the route taken by Kingcol and Habforce to reach Habbaniya – courtesy of and copyright Dr C D E Morris via RAF Habbaniya Association.

22. A hand drawn map detailing the Fallujah attack plan – from the collections of The National Archives (UK).

23. Balls! Daily Bulletin no. 16 – image of a document in and copyright CDW private collection.

24. The British Embassy under siege – photographer unknown, public domain.

25. Troops carrying a boat across Hammonds Bund – photographer unknown.

Acknowledgments

My thanks to Dr Christopher Morris of the RAF Habbaniya Association for kindly allowing me to use his images; to Mark Cremin, son of my father's flying instructor in Habbaniya, Dan Cremin, for a copy of the historical record of 'C' Squadron of the Habbaniya Air Striking Force that my father co-wrote at the time; to the staff at the National Archives at Kew for providing me with multiple files of background material; and to Wing Commander Mike Dudgeon, for his invaluable advice, and background on his father, Air-Vice Marshal Tony Dudgeon.

James Dunford Wood, London.

Made in the USA
Monee, IL
03 August 2024